SIMPLY HITCHCOCK

SIMPLY HITCHCOCK

DAVID STERRITT

Simply Charly

New York

Dedicated to Mikita,

Jeremy and Tanya,

Craig and Kim,

and Oliver, of course

Contents

Praise for *Simply Hitchcock*

"With his customary style and brilliance, David Sterritt neatly unpacks Hitchcock's long career with a sympathetic but sharply observant eye. As one of the cinema's most perceptive critics, Sterritt is uniquely qualified to write this concise and compact volume, which is the best quick overview of Hitchcock's work to date—written with both the cineaste and the general reader in mind. Rich in detail and observation, this is a book that unlocks the hidden terrain of Hitchcock's work, written with the lifetime experience of a master."

—**Wheeler Winston Dixon, author of** *Black and White Cinema: A Short History* **and Ryan Professor of Film Studies at the University of Nebraska, Lincoln**

"The faster the flow of publications on aspects of Hitchcock's work—specific films and themes and periods—the greater the need for a clear and concise overview of all that he did and of just what has made him into such a central figure. David Sterritt delivers precisely this, in a form that is thoughtful, readable, and cogent: it is an ideal primer on Hitchcock, and full of insights for those who think they know all about him already."

—**Charles Barr, author of** *Vertigo* **in the BFI Classics series and Emeritus Professor at the University of East Anglia**

"For everything you always wanted to know about Alfred Hitchcock, turn to David Sterritt who shares his extensive knowledge of the acclaimed director's life and career in an elegantly concise style. Simply put, this is a great book."

—**Jan Olsson, author of** *Hitchcock à la Carte* **and Professor in Cinema Studies at Stockholm University**

"David Sterritt packs incisive analyses of every Hitchcock film into a slim volume bursting with ideas, some startlingly new, others inventive variations on Hitchcock tropes. The result is a seasoned, highly readable exploration of Hitchcock as a whole—the myth, the reality, the major themes, the incomparable style, the personal idiosyncrasies, the staggeringly sustained achievement over six decades. Sterritt is especially deft at capturing Hitchcock's paradoxes: his casual juxtaposition of the ordinary with the exotic, the real with the surreal, the cerebral with the theatrical. There is not a better place to start for those who are new to Hitchcock, but Hitchcockians will merit by having a work that synthesizes all of Sterritt's well-known qualities—his elegance, erudition, and ability to pack complex ideas into entertaining commentaries. Like Hitchcock, Sterritt has the rare ability to speak to the specialist and the general audience. Not since Donald Spoto's *The Art of Alfred Hitchcock*, published well before academia's obsession with Hitchcock, has there been a work of such broad appeal."

—Jack Sullivan, author of *Hitchcock's Music*

"David Sterritt is widely recognized as one of the most knowledgeable, perceptive, and accessible commentators on Alfred Hitchcock's career. He makes a convincing case for the charm, technical innovativeness, and often perverse wit of Hitchcock's films and television shows while, at the same time, not shying away from exploring troubling aspects of his career. Relax with this delightful book and prepare for the illumination and sheer pleasure it delivers."

—William Luhr, author of *Thinking About Movies: Watching, Questioning, Enjoying* **and Professor of English at Saint Peter's University**

"Do we really need a new book on Hitchcock? David Sterritt shows that we do, as he brings his keen wit and penetrating intelligence to a study of the interconnections of Hitchcock's life and art. *Simply Hitchcock* is a kind of guidebook on the director's major themes that is both authoritative and fun to read."

—Christopher Sharrett, Professor of Visual and Sound Media at Seton Hall University

"*Simply Hitchcock* is an incisive introduction to the master's work. Erudite and accessible, Sterritt provides not only an overview of the career but vivid snapshots of the individual movies. The best way to read this book is alongside Hitchcock's films: watch one or two, referring to Sterritt's illuminating historical context as well as close analysis. Hitchcock set the standard for suspense, and this book helps us understand the reasons for his enduring impact."

—Annette Insdorf, author of *Francois Truffaut* and Professor of the Graduate Film Program & Director of Undergraduate Film Studies at Columbia University

"Concise, even-handed, and always as enjoyable as it is informative, *Simply Hitchcock* is the book to have in hand when beginning to explore the vast and often imposing territory of Alfred Hitchcock's life and works. David Sterritt handles the daunting task of surveying Hitchcock's career of more than 50 years and more than 50 films elegantly and efficiently. We learn what to watch for—including curiously attractive and sympathetic villains, vulnerable and beleaguered but complexly resourceful women, eroticized murders and murderous intimacies—even as we are advised to expect the unexpected from a filmmaker devoted to showing that the familiar is dangerous and strange. Well attuned to the technical virtuosity of one of cinema's great stylists and the philosophical depths of one of its great thinkers, Sterritt skillfully prepares his readers for the challenges and delights of Hitchcock's films, which he patiently demonstrates are evident in not only the acknowledged masterpieces but also in many of his lesser known films that readers of this book should—and undoubtedly will—immediately add to their viewing queue."

—Sidney Gottlieb, Professor of Communication and Media Studies, Sacred Heart University and Co-editor of the *Hitchcock Annual*

"It's hard to imagine a better introduction to the work of that most enduring and popular of film *auteurs* than *Simply Hitchcock*. David Sterritt gets the balance just right: one learns about the technician, the producer, the businessman, the media personality as well as the artist who created some of the richest, most profound works in the history of cinema. The tone is lively and engaging, and there's more than enough here to delight and surprise even those who swore they'd never read another word about Hitch."

—**Richard Peña, Professor of Film, Columbia University and former Director of the New York Film Festival**

Series Editor's Foreword

Simply Charly's "Great Lives" series offers brief but authoritative introductions to the world's most influential people—scientists, artists, writers, economists, and other historical figures whose contributions have had a meaningful and enduring impact on our society.

Each book provides an illuminating look at the works, ideas, personal lives, and the legacies these individuals left behind, also shedding light on the thought processes, specific events, and experiences that led these remarkable people to their groundbreaking discoveries or other achievements. Additionally, every volume explores various challenges they had to face and overcome to make history in their respective fields, as well as the little-known character traits, quirks, strengths, and frailties, myths and controversies that sometimes surrounded these personalities.

Our authors are prominent scholars and other top experts who have dedicated their careers to exploring each facet of their subjects' work and personal lives.

Unlike many other works that are merely descriptions of the major milestones in a person's life, the "Great Lives" series goes above and beyond the standard format and content. It brings substance, depth, and clarity to the sometimes-complex lives and works of history's most powerful and influential people.

We hope that by exploring this series, readers will not only gain new knowledge and understanding of what drove these geniuses, but also find inspiration for their own lives. Isn't this what a great book is supposed to do?

Charles Carlini, Simply Charly
New York City

.

Preface

Alfred Hitchcock was a legendary director, producer, impresario, entertainer, celebrity, and filmic philosopher. He was also an elegant host. On the weekly television program that bore his name, he welcomed viewers into every episode with a dignified "Good evening," followed by a wry little speech or mini-skit that connected in a whimsical way to the drama about to begin. In that spirit, I'll start this book about the Master of Suspense not in one of the places usually linked with him—his native England or his beloved Hollywood—but rather in the vaults of the New Zealand Film Archive, where a very Hitchcockian discovery made international news in 2010.

What researchers found there were three film reels that everyone thought had been lost, destroyed, or allowed to disintegrate decades earlier. The reels contained the first half of *The White Shadow*, a 1924 feature to which the 24-year-old Hitchcock, then a rising young talent in the British film industry, had energetically contributed.

It's hard to say exactly how footage from this English production ended up in a New Zealand film vault. But this was an era when movies were regarded as mere commodities, to be tossed in the rubbish when their commercial possibilities were exhausted. If a print was in the hands of a faraway exhibitor when its prospects ran dry, the distributor might see no point in paying for return shipping. New Zealand is a long way from London and Los Angeles, so it's easy to imagine a British or American company writing off copies of *The White Shadow* when no more theaters were in the market for them. A partly intact copy found its way to the New Zealand archive, where it was misidentified as an American movie—the titles and credits were missing, and it bore the mark of Lewis J. Selznick Enterprises, a Hollywood-based distributor—and stored under a generic title.

The White Shadow attracted enormous attention when the National Film Preservation Foundation (NFPF) in Washington, DC, brought the picture (and other works with American ties) from New Zealand to the United States, energetically publicizing the Hitchcock connection. Public excitement about the discovery testified to the continuing magic of Hitchcock's name—strong magic indeed, since only half of the movie was unearthed, and properly speaking, it isn't even a Hitchcock picture. He worked on it as an assistant to Graham Cutts, the veteran British filmmaker who actually directed it.

The important point here is Hitchcock's ability to make news 30 years after his death. Media outlets ranging from CNN to Radio Scotland and New Zealand's own Newstalk ZB covered the discovery of *The White Shadow*, and when the NFPF slated 176 recovered pictures for preservation to 35mm film and digital video, the opus by Cutts and Hitchcock was one of a dozen items released on a DVD called *Lost and Found: American Treasures from the New Zealand Film Archive*.[1] Shortly afterward it joined a longer list of selections streamed on the Internet for all to see. *The White Shadow* was out of the shadows for good, and admirers now hope the second half of the film will turn up in some other archive where it's been resting in obscurity since the age of silent cinema.

Turning to Hitchcock's career more broadly, his most famous contribution to the verbal lexicon of film is the word "MacGuffin," which he explained repeatedly over the years. In a 1968 essay he described it thus: "It's something that the characters in the film care a lot about, but the audience doesn't worry about it too much.... As a matter of fact I refuse to use the kind of thing [for MacGuffin material] which most people think is very important."[2]

Critics and scholars have glossed, paraphrased, and expanded on the word. Ken Mogg, editor of *The MacGuffin* and author of *The Alfred Hitchcock Story*, notes that it originated with Angus MacPhail, one of the director's screenwriter friends. Mogg continues:

The term [refers to] something that sets the film's plot revolving.... It's really just an excuse and a diversion. In a whimsical anecdote told by Hitchcock, he compared the MacGuffin to a mythical 'apparatus for trapping lions in the Scottish Highlands'. In other words, it could be anything—or nothing—at all. In *Notorious*, it's just a lot of fizz: uranium-ore hidden in [wine] bottles. In *North by Northwest*, it's 'government secrets', whatever they may be. (Hitchcock considered that this was his 'best' MacGuffin, because virtually non-existent.) Actually *North by Northwest* turns out to be one vast MacGuffin, being full of 'nothings' like the 'O' in Roger O. Thornhill's name, or the empty prairie, or the non-existent agent named Kaplan. In effect, the function of a MacGuffin is like the 'meaning' of a poem—which T.S. Eliot compared to the bone thrown by a burglar to distract the watchdog of the mind while the poem goes about its own, deeper business. Hitchcock's most prescient MacGuffin is in *Torn Curtain*, whose 'Gamma Five' project, concerning an anti-missile missile, anticipated by more than a decade President Reagan's 'Star Wars' project.[3]

Hitchcock's analysis was correct: something must be at stake for the people in the story, but for the audience that "something" matters far less than the challenges, relationships, triumphs, and defeats of the characters who experience them.

It's also true, however, that some moviegoers care more about narrative details than about character psychology. For them, the MacGuffin's inconsequentiality is a defect in Hitchcock's films. They want to know who put the uranium *into* the bottles in *Notorious*, what's *on* the strip of microfilm in *North by Northwest*, who *taught* the aircraft plans to Mr. Memory in *The 39 Steps*, just *how* Harry died in *The Trouble with Harry*, and for *what* possible reason *The Birds* are suddenly attacking the human race. Hitchcock had a word for moviegoers like these: he called them "Plausibles," and he didn't hold their opinions in high regard. For him, it was pointless to fuss over details that don't seem "realistic," as if *anything* is truly "realistic" in a motion picture, that artificial beast with two dimensions and straight-edged borders.

Hitchcock dismissed such nitpicking cheerfully and also thoughtfully. "I'm not concerned with plausibility," he told French film director François Truffaut in one of their interview sessions; "that's the easiest part of it, so why bother?" He then remarked on the imperatives of *his* kind of cinema, contrasting the Hitchcock approach with the documentary method that had influenced but not taken over his style:

> There's quite a difference, you see, between the creation of a film and the making of a documentary. In the documentary, the basic material has been created by God, whereas in the fiction film the director is the god; he must create life. And in the process of that creation, there are lots of feelings, forms of expression, and viewpoints that have to be juxtaposed. We should have total freedom to do as we like, just so long as it's not dull. A critic who talks to me about plausibility is a dull fellow.[4]

On another occasion, he summed it up in a sentence: "For me, the cinema is not a slice of life, but a piece of cake."[5]

Acknowledgements

Thanks to all the critics, scholars, cinephiles, and friends who have enriched my appreciation of Alfred Hitchcock's work through books, essays, articles, and discussions for lo these many decades. Naming them all is impossible, but the most insightful in their views and helpful to my thinking include Sid Gottlieb, Tom Doherty, Chris Sharrett, Bill Luhr, Tom Leitch, Pat McGilligan, Jan Olsson, James Naremore, Richard Allen, Bill Rothman, Andrew Sarris, Donald Spoto, Paula Marantz Cohen, Lesley Brill, Christopher Brookhouse, Robin Wood, and many more. Special thanks to the exemplary Hitchcock scholar Charles Barr for advice way above the call of duty, and to Charles Carlini for inviting me to embark on this enjoyable project.

1

Hitch

What accounts for the power and persistence of the Hitchcock mystique? What's the breadth and depth of his appeal, which reaches out to moviegoers of every kind, from Saturday-night entertainment seekers to connoisseurs of cinematic art?

There's no single answer to those questions, no unified theory to explain Hitchcock's popularity. One reason for his enduring sway is the consistency of his commitment to the suspense film, a genre that's both perennially alluring and flexible enough to accommodate changing public tastes in movie style and content.

Another is his ability to deploy iconic movie stars in ways that either foreground their most charismatic traits—think Cary Grant's inextinguishable charm in *Notorious* (1946) and *North by Northwest* (1959), or Grace Kelly in *Rear Window* (1954) and *To Catch a Thief* (1955)—or play them daringly against type, as James Stewart does in *Rope* (1948) and *Vertigo* (1958) and Doris Day does in *The Man Who Knew Too Much* (1956). Still another is the remarkable durability of his own celebrity image, which he devised and cultivated as ingeniously as he designed, crafted, and promoted his films, television shows, and public appearances. To this day, his doughy face and fleshy figure are instantly recognizable symbols of mainstream entertainment with a thrilling, romantic tang.

In my view, though, the most important single factor in Hitchcock's unending popularity is something more profound—his never-ending fascination with the unresolvable tension between order and chaos, a fundamental concern of modern art and of modern life. Hitchcock was sometimes explicit about this, as when he acknowledged that *The Birds* (1963) is meant to show anarchic turmoil overtaking the forces

1

of regularity, stability, and predictability that we normally take for granted in the world; this usurpation of power may be the inevitable outcome of humanity's "messing about" with the age-old balances of our natural environment, but it may just as easily be something else, or—the most frightening prospect—it might be caused by nothing we can explain, or understand, or even know.[1]

The danger of being thrust from the everyday world into a chaos world (to borrow critic Robin Wood's suggestive term) was a philosophical issue of deep interest for the filmmaker.[2] It was also a psychological and spiritual issue that stirred him to his bones. The threat, the likelihood, or even the possibility of a plunge into disorder, turmoil, anarchy, or madness was never far from his thoughts, as both his movies and his biography attest. He appears to have lived, labored, and dreamed in a state of half-repressed anxiety that was no less visceral for being largely bottled up behind a double façade of traditional British propriety and up-to-the-minute American achievement. Creative work was his safety valve, and the ability to communicate his half-hidden fears in universally meaningful forms was his saving grace.

Soviets, documentaries, and the London Film Society

Many factors played into the evolution of Hitchcock's audiovisual style. Perhaps the most significant was the theory of film editing put forward by pioneering Soviet filmmakers—Sergei M. Eisenstein, Vsevolod Pudovkin, Aleksandr Dovzhenko, Dziga Vertov—in the 1920s. The greatest of these trailblazers was Eisenstein, who believed that individual shots should not follow each other like links in a chain but should *contrast*, *conflict with*, and even *contradict* one another from moment to moment, encouraging active thought in the spectator and offering visual excitement on the screen. A marvelous example of how brilliantly Hitchcock used this technique is the opening sequence of *Strangers on a Train*, where shots of walking feet build up a tense yet humorous rhythm while introducing the main characters and foreshadowing the role that chance and synchronicity will play in the story to come.

Hitchcock also embraced what film scholars call the Kuleshov effect, named after Lev Kuleshov's experiments with the ordering of shots to produce particular reactions in the audience. Hitchcock concisely explained this in a 1964 television appearance, linking it to the "pure cinematics" that he valued so highly:

> I have a close-up [of a character's face]. Now I show what he sees, and let's assume he sees a woman holding a baby in her arms. Now we cut back to his reaction to what he sees, and he smiles. Now what is he, as a character? He's a kindly man; he's sympathetic. Now let's take the middle piece of film away—the woman with the child—but leave his two pieces of film as they were. And we'll put in a piece of film with a girl in a bikini. He looks ... he smiles. What is he now? A dirty old man, no longer the benign gentleman who loves babies! That's what film can do for you.[3]

Rear Window most famously displays Kuleshov's influence on Hitchcock as it cuts between what the main character *sees* and how he *reacts* to what he sees. But instances can be found in nearly all Hitchcock films, with the notable exception of *Rope*, in which the director experimented with an opposite technique, replacing normal shot-by-shot editing with unusually long takes, strategic camera movements, and hidden cuts disguised by objects blocking the frame. The results of that experiment were unsatisfactory, most notably to Hitchcock himself.[4]

Hitchcock spent many hours at screenings held by the London Film Society, where such innovative Soviet features as Eisenstein's *Battleship Potemkin* (1925) and Pudovkin's *Mother* (1926) could be seen and studied. The lessons he learned from Soviet montage stayed with him forever. When the Film Society of Lincoln Center devoted its annual gala tribute to him in 1974, a reel of Hitchcockian highlights brought together some of his most famous scenes, including the part of *Dial M for Murder* where Margot Mary Wendice (Grace Kelly) defends her life by killing Captain Lesgate (Anthony Dawson) with a pair of scissors. At the close of the tribute, Hitchcock gave his thank-you speech not in person (like recipients in other years) but on the screen, in a brief monologue filmed at Universal a few days earlier. When it was over, he rose in his box seat and spoke to the cheering audience: "As you have seen on the screen, scissors are the best way." He was referring to Margot's successful self-defense, of course, but he was also tipping his hat to the power of film editing, which he exploited as effectively as any director ever has.

Even as he studied the Soviet style, Hitchcock was fascinated by documentaries. Incorporating elements of realistic, documentary-like detail was a way of grounding the extreme, even bizarre aspects of his stories—the murders, misapprehensions, deceptions, chases, evasions, escapes, and so on—in the day-to-day realities of his audience, thus enhancing his films' ability to push emotional buttons and make spectators squirm with suspense. In a 1937 article for *Kine Weekly*, Hitchcock spelled out his desire to put middle-class citizens, "that vital central stratum of British humanity," onto the big screen. As a bonus, he hoped his fine-grained portraits of commonplace people and places would help him appeal more strongly to the vast American marketplace. Ideally, he wrote, he would "do unto America what they have done unto us, and make the cheerful man and girl of our middle class as colorful and dramatic to them as their ordinary everyday citizens are to the audiences of England."[5]

That was Hitchcock's stated aim in the 1930s, and his early films attest to his sincerity; as examples, the British critic and filmmaker Lindsay Anderson pointed to such gritty, workaday details as the restaurant and tobacco shops in *Blackmail*, the chapel in the first version of *The Man Who Knew Too Much*, the country house in *The 39 Steps*, and the movie house in *Sabotage*. Hitchcock never lost his mischievous wish to bring crime, violence, and menace out of the shadows and dark alleys and into the bright light of day. Think of Roger Thornhill running for his life through a Midwestern wheat field in *North by Northwest*, or the deadly assault in a dating-service office at lunchtime in *Frenzy*, or Marion Crane's bloody murder in a sanitary motel bathroom in *Psycho*, and Hitchcock's artful blending of the real and the outlandish stands out in high relief.

Influences from UFA and America
Hitchcock was similarly impressed with works by the expressionist

filmmakers in Germany, such as Robert Wiene's *The Cabinet of Dr. Caligari* (1919) and Fritz Lang's *Dr. Mabuse: The Gambler* (1922), which tell stories of physical danger and mental derangement—as an offshoot of the Romantic movement, expressionism thrived on anything extreme, uncontrolled, or uncontrollable—through deliberately exaggerated visuals akin to those of Surrealist art. Expressionism strongly influenced the Hollywood horror films of the 1930s, the film-noir cycle of the 1940s and 1950s, and such enduring Hitchcock classics as *The Lodger*, with its fog-shrouded atmosphere and hallucinatory shot of the title character's feet pacing above a transparent ceiling, and *Spellbound*, where Ballantyne's revelatory nightmare is evoked through Salvador Dalí's dreamlike set designs.

Hitchcock's aesthetics were greatly affected by his experiences at Universum Film AG, better known as UFA, the towering German studio that nurtured such important and influential filmmakers as F.W. Murnau, Fritz Lang, William Dieterle, Ernst Lubitsch, and Robert Siodmak, to mention only directors who emigrated to the United States in the 1920s or 1930s and worked in the Hollywood system. (Leni Riefenstahl and Veit Harlan, who emerged in the 1930s and became notorious for their Nazi connections, are among the directors who stayed put.) An array of luminous stars—Marlene Dietrich, Emil Jannings, Pola Negri, Rudolf Klein-Rogge, Brigitte Helm, Conrad Veidt—also created major performances at UFA during the silent and early sound-film eras.

Hitchcock worked there on *The Blackguard* when the likes of Lang and Jannings were active and Murnau was making his 1924 classic *The Last Laugh*, which Hitchcock later called "almost the perfect film," noting in particular—long before the term "pure cinema" entered his vocabulary—that it "told its story ... entirely by the use of imagery." He spent an afternoon observing and talking with Murnau, who explained how he used forced perspective to make a setting look more extensive than it actually was, and how a particular aspect of design—in this case, lines converging in the direction of a large railway-station clock—could both accentuate an element of décor (the clock) and suggest an unspoken or symbolic meaning (the significance of time). According to biographer Donald Spoto, these hours with Murnau influenced Hitchcock's designs for *The Blackguard* the following day.[6]

In time to come, Hitchcock acknowledged that *The Lodger*, his breakthrough picture, displayed "a very Germanic influence … in lighting and setting and everything else."[7] Many other Hitchcock films, from *Rich and Strange* (1931) and *Sabotage* to *The Wrong Man* and *Psycho*, bear similarly forceful evidence of the impact German silent cinema exerted on him. "My models were forever after the German filmmakers of 1924 and 1925," he said of the lessons UFA taught. "They were trying very hard to express ideas in purely visual terms."[8]

American talents and techniques affected the young Hitchcock as well. His admiration of American directors dated from his viewings of D.W. Griffith's major epics—*The Birth of a Nation* (1915), *Intolerance: Love's Struggle Throughout the Ages* (1916), *Way Down East* (1920)—and Charles Chaplin's winsome comedies, among which *The Pilgrim* (1923) was a favorite. American techniques started to influence him the moment he walked into British Famous Players-Lasky for his first job in the movie business. As the British branch of an American company, this enterprising studio aimed to showcase British subjects, themes, and personalities in pictures given an extra boost by American know-how and technical expertise.

Directors like George Fitzmaurice and John S. Robertson, writers like Jeanie Macpherson and Tom Geraghty, and many of the technicians had Hollywood credentials, and cameras and other equipment were American imports as well. Hitchcock had high regard for the sophisticated lighting, sense of photographic depth, and overall technical excellence of American movies, and he similarly admired the resourceful ideas of the "middle-aged American women," as he called them, who dominated the studio's scenario department. From them, he learned to "focus on actresses, emphasize the female characters, accent their performances, highlight their appearances," in biographer Patrick McGilligan's words, and "to have women surrounding him to help toward that goal."[9]

Themes and motifs…

In a landmark volume called *Hitchcock*, first published in 1957, the

young French film critics Claude Chabrol and Éric Rohmer set forth
the first book-length study of the stories, themes, and techniques that
transform Hitchcock's movies from a string of merely entertaining
thrillers into a sustained exploration of what it means to be human
in a world where hopes and ambitions are so frequently outrun by
misgivings, trepidations, and fears. Chabrol and Rohmer soon moved
into their own illustrious careers as charter members of the
revolutionary French New Wave, but many other critics have
continued the work they so brilliantly began, teasing out and
elaborating on the sophisticated pleasures and resonant ideas of
Hitchcock's cinematic universe. Here's a quick look at some of the
most important motifs that thread their way through almost every
Hitchcock film, with brief examples for each:

The haziness of the lines that supposedly separate good from evil
Lifeboat (1944): The assorted American and British passengers seem
very different from the German enemies who sank their ship, but
the differences fade when they're betrayed by a German captain they
rescued.

Rope (1948): The schoolmaster taught his students to toy with
murderous ideas, and now he's shocked, shocked that they acted on
what they learned.

The difficulty of distinguishing the guilty from the innocent
The Lodger: A Story of the London Fog (1927): A mysterious stranger
(Ivor Novello) rents a room in a nice old couple's house and becomes
the chief suspect in neighborhood murders that *he* is trying to solve.

Spellbound (1945): Almost everyone thinks John Ballantyne (Gregory
Peck) is a murderer, including John Ballantyne himself, but his
psychiatrist (Ingrid Bergman) is convinced he's completely innocent.

The transference of guilt from a wrongdoer to someone else
Blackmail (1929): After she kills a man who tried to rape her, Alice's

policeman boyfriend protects her by letting a sleazy ex-convict fall under suspicion for the slaying.

Shadow of a Doubt (1943): Learning that her visiting uncle is a serial killer, Young Charlie (Teresa Wright) hides the truth to preserve her mother's peace of mind, which means *she* will be responsible if he murders again.

Seeing is very, very powerful...
Young and Innocent (1937): Erica (Nova Pilbeam) recognizes the villain by spotting his telltale twitch, twitch, twitch.

Foreign Correspondent (1940): Holland is full of windmills, but ace reporter John Jones (Joel McCrea) locates the spies by observing a peculiar characteristic of the one in which they're hiding.

...but seeing is very, very unreliable...
North by Northwest: You can see Roger O. Thornhill (Grant) in the front-page photo, standing over the corpse with the knife in his hand, but he had nothing to do with the murder.

Marnie (1964): In the first scene she's a brazen dark-haired burglar, but by the end, she's the opposite in all three departments, and the latter Marnie is at least as authentic as the former one.

...and voyeurism is a very tempting vice
Rear Window (1954): Housebound with a broken leg, Jeff (James Stewart) spies on his neighbors via the eponymous window pane, finding clues that one of them might have murdered his wife.

Psycho (1960): Norman (Anthony Perkins) spying on Marion (Janet Leigh) in the shower is an iconic image—perhaps *the* iconic image—in modern cinema.

Doubles, doppelgängers, and dead ringers
The Wrong Man (1957): Manny Balestrero (Henry Fonda) is accused

of robberies committed by a lookalike he never met, and the criminal-justice system turns his life into a nightmare.

Vertigo (1958): Scottie (Stewart) falls passionately in love twice over, first with glamorous blonde Madeleine Elster (Kim Novak) and then with working-class brunette Judy Barton (Novak), realizing too late that they're far more similar than they appear.

Knowledge = Danger

The 39 Steps (1935): Richard Hannay (Robert Donat) leads a contented life until Annabella Smith (Lucie Mannheim) tells him a secret of national importance and then dies, leaving him to expose an espionage ring while dodging police who blame him for Annabella's death.

The Man Who Knew Too Much (1934 and 1956): A stranger tells a vacationing couple about an assassination plot, and they have to prevent the killing themselves in order to save their kidnapped child.

Theatricality, performance, making a scene!

Murder! (1930): The famous impresario (Herbert Marshall) confirms his suspicions by enticing the killer (Esme Percy) into reenacting the crime in an "audition," and the criminal then meets his doom in a suicidal circus act.

Stage Fright (1950): Eve (Jane Wyman) works to clear her friend's name by masquerading as a maid, capping the imposture by literally throwing a fit.

The police aren't bad...

Dial M for Murder (1954): The doggedness of Chief Inspector Hubbard (John Williams) pays off, giving him good reason to smile as he combs his mustache at the end.

Frenzy (1972): Having cracked the case, Chief Inspector Oxford (Alec McCowen) deadpans one of Hitchcock's wryest lines when he says, "Mr. Rusk, you're not wearing your tie."

...they're just ineffectual, or scary, or both

Rope (1948): On the street below, a policeman ushers some kids across the street; behind the window above, a murder is happening, and the minion of the law is oblivious.

To Catch a Thief (1955): Reformed cat burglar John Robie (Grant) must find the copycat who's using his old methods, and meanwhile, he must dodge the police, who think it's not a copycat but Robie back to his bad habits.

Putting the audience in the bad guy's shoes

Strangers on a Train (1951): Bruno Anthony (Robert Walker) must retrieve the incriminating lighter he's dropped through a sewer grating, and although he's definitely a psychopath, you can't help empathizing with his stretching, straining fingers as they reach closer and closer without ... quite ... quite ... grasping ... it ... yet ...

Notorious (1946): You have to sympathize a tiny bit with Alex (Claude Rains) when he's forced to reenter the house and face the deadly consequences of his failure to advance the Nazi cause. Worse yet, he has to face his mother.

...and fetishes and phobias

Those and other themes appear and reappear throughout Hitchcock's body of work, sometimes subtly, sometimes not. Some crop up so often that it's reasonable to assume they reflect fetishes and phobias that Hitchcock harbored in his own mind and heart. They often intersect and overlap, moreover, forming patterns charged with great expressive force, as when the voyeurism theme connects with his penchant for putting the spectator in emotional cahoots with the villain. Never once have I seen viewers decorously avert their eyes when Norman ogles Marion in the shower, or Jeff peeps at private moments across the courtyard, or Scottie snoops on Madeleine's peregrinations. And recall the moment when Norman pushes Marion's car (containing Marion's body) into the swamp, where it sinks and sinks ... until it stops, leaving the vehicle's roof exposed and plain to see. Has there ever been a moviegoer who doesn't bristle nervously along with Norman, then breathe a sigh of relief when it finally goes gurgling all the way down? In addition to the major themes that Hitchcock perennially explores, he often punctuates his films with signs and symbols conveying personal, semi-private feelings in a kind of visual shorthand all his own. In doing this, he is not just indulging momentary whims. He is developing a coherent set of leitmotifs that appear and reappear, forming patterns and taking on meanings that viewers can infer and interpret as they watch, thereby enhancing their comprehension and appreciation of his works.

The signs and symbols carrying strong psychological charges for Hitchcock include:

Birds – Our feathered "friends" signaled danger and distress in Hitchcock's movies long before *The Birds* made it official in 1963. His first sound film, *Blackmail*, has one of his first great sound effects—a caged bird chirping away in Alice's bedroom just when the traumatized young woman desperately needs quiet—and his last film, *Family Plot*, shows old Julia *Rainbird* (Cathleen Nesbitt) consulting with a psychic. The bomb in *Sabotage* (1936) is hidden in a canary cage, and the motel office in *Psycho* is a veritable museum of avian taxidermy, inhabited by a man with birdlike mannerisms and visited by a woman named Marion *Crane* who comes from *Phoenix* and eats *like a bird*.

Blondes – Light-haired women crop up almost everywhere. Among them are chorus girls in *The Pleasure Garden* (1925), Daisy Bunting (June Tripp, credited by her first name only) in *The Lodger*, Brenda Blaney (Barbara Leigh-Hunt) in *Frenzy*, and Blanche Tyler (Barbara Harris) in *Family Plot* (1976), which also shows Fran (Karen Black) disguised with a blond wig. When other colorings appear they tend toward brunette rather than raven-dark—Iris Henderson (Margaret Lockwood) in *The Lady Vanishes* (1938), Alicia Huberman (Bergman) in *Notorious*—and redheads like Lady Henrietta Flusky (Bergman) in *Under Capricorn* (1949) and Jennifer Rogers (Shirley MacLaine) in *The Trouble with Harry* (1955) also turn up on occasion. The quintessential Hitchcock heroine is Grace Kelly in *Dial M for Murder*, *Rear Window* and *To Catch a Thief*, in which she is unfailingly suave, unruffled, and dazzlingly blonde.

Food, glorious food – It is hardly surprising that a man with Hitchcock's affection for eating would place a variety of meals, from banquets to picnics, into his films. Some are appetizing, and others are unsavory because of ingredients or presentation; instances of the latter include the queasy-making French meals cooked by Mrs. Oxford (Vivien Merchant) in *Frenzy* and the buffet served off a corpse-concealing trunk in *Rope*, and *To Catch a Thief* contains both a nice-looking quiche Lorraine and an unfortunate fried egg in which Jessie Stevens (Jessie Royce Landis) amusingly scrunches out a cigarette. In a French book on Hitchcockian cuisine, *The Sauce Was Nearly Perfect: 80 Recipes from Alfred Hitchcock*, the cinematically minded gourmets Anne Martinetti and François Rivière tell how to make a Scotland Yard breakfast inspired by Inspector Oxford's preferred repast in *Frenzy*; a Moroccan tagine *à la* the second version of *The Man Who Knew Too Much*; blueberry muffins like those seen when Ivy Gravely and Captain Wiles talk in *The Trouble with Harry*; a girly-pink birthday cake as in *The Birds*; foodstuffs seen in *Vertigo* (Maryland turkey supreme), *Marnie* (pecan pie), *North by Northwest* (trout), and *Rebecca* (plum bread), plus a leg of lamb in homage to "Lamb to the Slaughter" (1958), an episode of *Alfred Hitchcock Presents* about a scorned wife with an unusual murder weapon, directed by Hitchcock himself.[10] Many others can be added. Feast your eyes.

From the heights to the depths: falling, plunging, plummeting – "I look up, I look down. I look up, I look down." Scottie optimistically repeats that mantra in *Vertigo*, gradually ascending a ladder and persuading himself that his acrophobia can be swept away like a mental cobweb—a mistaken notion, as he discovers when a sidelong glance out a window sends him into a dead faint. Set amid the ups and down of hilly San Francisco, *Vertigo* is Hitchcock's ultimate dissertation on high and low as metaphors with an enormous range of meanings throughout his body of films: danger and safety, excitement and exhaustion, romance and rejection, idealism and cynicism, spirituality and materiality, life and death. Good people endangered by heights include Roger drunk behind the wheel in *North by Northwest*, George Lumley and Blanche careening with no brakes in *Family Plot*, the blameless Caypor (Percy Marmont) climbing the mountain in *Secret Agent* (1936), Jefferies at the climax of *Rear Window*, and Detective Arbogast at the top of the stairs in *Psycho*. Bad people imperiled by elevations include Tracy (Donald Calthorp) in the British Museum in *Blackmail*, the mad Sir Humphrey Pengallan (Charles Laughton) atop a ship's mast in *Jamaica Inn* (1939), Frank Fry (Norman Lloyd) atop the Statue of Liberty in *Saboteur* (1942), and Handel Fane on a fatal trapeze in *Murder!* At times, symbolic meanings of high and low lose their usual differences. Falls kill both the brave police officer and the deceitful Madeleine in *Vertigo*, for instance; and while the most spectacular catastrophe in *The Birds* is the horrifying explosion of a car, one of those intrinsically earthbound vehicles also takes Melanie and the Brenner family toward (ambiguous) safety at the end. Like so much else, heights and depths are richly ambiguous in Hitchcock's cinema.

Newspapers – Critics have paid little attention to the many newspapers in Hitchcock's films. Sometimes a paper displays a minor detail—at one point in *Murder!* a small advertisement fills the screen—but sometimes big news is breaking, as when Roger Thornhill brandishing a knife becomes a front-page photo in *North by Northwest*. Uncle Charlie of *Shadow of a Doubt* clips out a damning article so that the family won't read about his murderous past, and young Charlie visits the library to find the article and confirm the fears that haunt her. The eponymous *Foreign Correspondent* works for the *New York Globe*, and in *Easy Virtue* (1928) divorcée Larita Filton (Isabel Jeans) is speaking to news photographers when she utters her exit line, "Shoot! There's nothing left to kill." A rolled-up newspaper hides Marion's stolen money in *Psycho*, and it's still there when Norman heedlessly tosses the paper away. The most ingenious use of newsprint may be in *Lifeboat*, where the isolated setting posed a problem for the director's customary cameo appearance until he found an ideal vehicle: on a newspaper floating with the flotsam of a sunken ship, an ad displays him in the "Before" and "After" stages of a weight-reducing diet.

Newspaper scribes expended plenty of ink on Hitchcock in his day, and it's fair to say that he repaid the favor.

Handcuffs – Hitchcock was candid about the lure of handcuffs, saying that being manacled or tied is "somewhere in the area of fetishism." And not just for him. Arguing that they have an inherent "sexual connotation," he recalled visiting a vice museum in Paris and observing "considerable evidence of sexual aberrations through restraint."[11] Accordingly, his most memorable handcuff images appear in scenes involving romance and sexuality, when a person is handcuffed not just to some*thing*—as in *Saboteur* when Pat (Priscilla Lane) chains Barry (Robert Cummings) to her car with cuffs—but to some*one*. Exhibit A is the portion of *The 39 Steps* where accused killer Richard Hannay (Robert Donat) and unwilling companion Pamela (Madeleine Carroll) are forcefully connected by cuffs, greatly distressing Pamela until new information reveals Hannay's innocence and propinquity nudges them toward love. Hitchcock's interest in handcuffs is also obvious in *Blackmail*, where they dangle aggressively in the foreground as the police process a criminal. Their sexy-sinister overtones emerge as early as *The Lodger*, where police detective Joe interrupts his hunt for the murderous Avenger long enough to tell his girlfriend Daisy that he'll put a ring on her finger once he's put a noose around the killer's neck, using his handcuffs as a prop to dramatize his determination to snare the villain, and—patriarchal sexist that he is—to snare Daisy in the same possessive spirit. The climax of *The Lodger* highlights the shifting symbolism of wrist restraints, as handcuffs pinion the falsely vilified Jonathan to a pointed fence post while a furious crowd seethes around him; the crowd sees his cuffs as badges of guilt, but we can see him as a Christ figure suffering humiliation and possible martyrdom for sins he never committed. The many meanings of handcuffs carry over to other kinds of Hitchcockian bondage and restraint, from the cord encircling the books in *Rope* to the necktie strangler's weapon in *Frenzy*. The ties that bind aren't always blessed.

Moms and dads – Critics have paid attention to mothers in Hitchcock's films, and rightly so. There are plenty of them, and they often fall noticeably short in the traits traditionally associated with cinematic moms: nurture, guidance, protection, warmth, even basic parental love. A few are brave and selfless, like the kidnaped boy's mother in both versions of *The Man Who Knew Too Much*; or solid and trustworthy like Mama Balestrero (Esther Minciotti) in *The Wrong Man*; but they are exceptions. More typical are ridiculous ones like Mrs. Antony (Marion Lorne) in *Strangers on a Train* and Mrs. Rusk (Rita Webb) in *Frenzy*; clueless ones like Emma Newton (Patricia Collinge) in *Shadow of a Doubt* and Clara Thornhill in *North by Northwest*; troubled ones like Lydia Brenner (Jessica Tandy) in *The Birds* and Bernice Edgar (Louise Latham) in *Marnie*; and malignant ones like Mme. Sebastian (Madame Konstantin) in *Notorious* and the late Mrs. Bates in *Psycho*. Less notice has been paid to Hitchcock's fathers, and this too makes sense, for they're generally a less striking crowd, especially in the American phase of his career. The film scholar Tom Ryall points to harsh fathers in early films like *Downhill* (1927), *Champagne* (1928), *The Manxman* (1929), and *Waltzes from Vienna* (1934), and unlikable ones in the 1930s thrillers *Young and Innocent*, *The 39 Steps*, and *The Lady Vanishes*; and Ryall fleshes out the roster with the treacherous step-father in *Sabotage* and unsympathetic father figures in *Lifeboat*, *Saboteur*, and *Foreign Correspondent* (1940).[12] Some other Hitchcock films have fathers who don't do much fathering, like Manny Balestrero, whose legal struggles in *The Wrong Man* leave little time for the kids. Elsewhere, dads seem nondescript, like the dull Joseph Newton (Henry Travers) in *Shadow of a Doubt* and the duller Mr. Kentley (Sir Cedric Hardwicke) in *Rope*. And often dads are absent altogether, like the late Mr. Bates of *Psycho* and the late Mr. Brenner of *The Birds*. Parents provide little comfort or protection in Hitchcock's dangerous world.

Stairs – The title of *The 39 Steps* has a literal meaning in the novel by John Buchan on which Hitchcock's film is based: the steps are a stairway leading from a country house to a private beach below. The phrase refers to something quite different in the movie, becoming a metaphor that punctuates the surprise ending and encapsulates the arduous difficulties that Hannay has scrambled over in the course of solving the mystery and defeating the foe. Actual stairways figure prominently in many Hitchcock films, however, acquiring an array of psychological and emotional resonances. *Psycho* contains the most familiar examples—the stone steps rising from the desolate motel to the spooky house, the staircase on which Arbogast meets his doom, the stairs that Lila (Vera Miles) descends to the forbidding fruit cellar. The bell-tower stairs in *Vertigo* are equally significant, as are the stairs in *Notorious, from* which the camera tracks toward a crucial detail in a crowded scene and *down* which Devlin carries Alicia (Bergman) as their enemies look on. Other memorable steps include the fire escape that Lisa (Kelly) climbs in *Rear Window*, the outdoor stairway that a diplomat tumbles down after being shot in *Foreign Correspondent*, the stairway rug that conceals a key in *Dial M for Murder*, and the stairs in the home of Bruno's parents in *Strangers on a Train*, guarded by a baleful dog, a Cerberus of the American upper class.

Trains – The climaxes of *Number Seventeen* (1932) and *Secret Agent* (1936) are spectacular train crashes. In *The Lady Vanishes*, Miss Froy (Dame May Whitty) suddenly disappears during a voyage on a train. Uncle Charlie (Joseph Cotten) rides into *Shadow of a Doubt* on a train, puffing dark Satanic smoke as it pulls into the Santa Rosa station, and he fittingly meets his doom on one as well. Roger Thornhill and Eve Kendall (Eva Marie Saint) meet on the 20th Century Limited in *North by Northwest*, and when Hannay's housekeeper discovers a corpse in *The 39 Steps*, we see her scream but hear the whistle of the Flying Scotsman, the train on which Hannay is already fleeing northward to evade pursuit. Although it spends little time actually on the rails, *Strangers on a Train* uses intersecting tracks to symbolize intersecting lives. One of Hitchcock's youthful hobbies was memorizing railway timetables, and one feels the lure of the locomotive in many of his films.

Alma Reville

As mentioned earlier, Hitchcock learned from his mentors that having women around him in the studio helped him refine his ongoing effort to focus on actresses and emphasize his female characters. By far the most important woman he kept near him was Alma Reville, whom he met at the Gainsborough studio in 1920 and married six years later. She was just one day older than her future husband, but despite their nearly identical ages, he was still working on intertitles in 1920, whereas she had five years of film experience, first as a tea girl and then as a secretary, editor, and scenario writer. At first, she worked for other directors as well as Hitchcock, but she soon became his key collaborator, engaged in nearly every aspect of his productions, from finding stories to location scouting, casting, suggesting visual ideas, and inspecting processed footage. She was an ideal successor to the American women who had helped shape Hitchcock's sensibilities at British Famous Players-Lasky, and looking at pictures in which Reville receives a screenplay or adaptation credit, film historian Josephine Botting observes that a striking number contain "strong, well-drawn female roles," as do movies like Adrian Brunel's *The Constant Nymph* (1928) and Maurice Elvey's *The Water Gipsies* (1935), as well as Hitchcock's own *Suspicion* (1941), *The Paradine Case* (1949), and *Stage Fright* (1949).[13] Reville died in 1982, and *Los Angeles Times* film critic Charles Champlin memorialized her inestimable contributions when he wrote that "the Hitchcock touch had four hands" and two of them belonged to his gifted wife.[14] Three years before her death Hitchcock had paid his own heartfelt tribute when accepting the American Film Institute Life Achievement Award. "Among those many people who have contributed to my life," he said in part,

> I ask permission to mention by name only four people who have given me the most affection, appreciation and encouragement, and constant collaboration. The first of the four is a film editor. The second is a scriptwriter. The third is the mother of my daughter, Pat. And the fourth is as fine a cook as ever performed miracles in a domestic kitchen. And their names are Alma Reville.

With characteristic humor, Hitchcock added that if Reville had not "accepted a lifetime contract without options" as his wife 53 years earlier, he might be present at the award ceremony "not at this table, but as one of the slower waiters on the floor."[15]

2

Silents Are Golden

A lfred Hitchcock was born into a middle-class Roman Catholic family in London on August 13, 1899, just as the Victorian era was approaching its end. His father, William, dealt in poultry and fruit, and his mother, Emma, tended the home. The youngest of three children, Alfred developed a secret bingeing habit and became seriously overweight early on; his girth contributed to his sense of loneliness and isolation. His childhood was not happy in other ways as well, marred by punishments doled out by his strict parents: at the age of five, for example, his father sent him to a police station to be locked up in a cell after the youngster misbehaved. Hitchcock claimed that this experience, and others like it, fed his lifelong interest in the subjects of guilt, unfair treatment, and wrongful accusations—themes that would later figure prominently in his films. (Not surprisingly, Hitchcock developed a lifelong fear of authority figures and, stranger still, he was also afraid of eggs, famously saying, "I'm frightened of eggs, worse than frightened; they revolt me."

Young Alfred attended a Jesuit high school and then worked in the sales and advertising departments of a telegraph company while studying design, drawing, and electrical engineering on the side. But he had an artistic side as well, developing an early taste for literature (Charles Dickens, Gustave Flaubert, Edgar Allan Poe) and the theater (J.M. Barrie, Henrik Ibsen, John Galsworthy). He also became interested in cinema, which came into existence just a few years before he did.

In his early 20s, Hitchcock landed a job with the British branch of an American film company, Famous Players-Lasky, designing the intertitles that provide bits of dialogue and information in silent movies; he earned his first screen credit for crafting the title cards of Hugh Ford's drama *The Great Day* (1920), which has no other claim to fame. Famous Players-Lasky shuttered its British office a couple of years later, but Hitchcock stayed in the industry, knowing he had found his calling in life. Before long he was writing, designing, editing, and helping to direct entire films, learning on the job and soon surpassing some of the professionals who trained him.

Cutts

One of those early productions was *The White Shadow*, the second of three pictures released by the London production company Balcon, Freedman & Saville during its brief lifespan. It was also the third of five pictures that Hitchcock worked on as an assistant to director Graham Cutts, and looking at its history gives a good idea of what Britain's film industry was like when Hitch broke into it.

Cutts was a very reputable director, older than Hitchcock by 14 years. He had started his career in 1909 as an exhibitor—proclaimed "the master showman of the North" by producer-director Herbert Wilcox, who became his business partner—and made his directorial debut with *The Wonderful Story*, a 1922 melodrama marked by "truth, realism and perfect acting," in the eyes of a *Kinematograph Weekly* critic. His subsequent films of the decade were widely hailed for "spectacular production values, experimental virtuosity of camerawork and lighting and the intense performances and attractive characterisations of his actors, several of whom rose to stardom under his direction," according to film historian Christine Gledhill, who adds that Cutts employed "the voyeuristic potential of the camera to explore subjectivity and sexuality," much as Hitchcock would eventually do.[1]

In addition to his directorial talents, Cutts had a busy romantic life. This tended to distract him from his filmmaking duties, opening opportunities for Hitchcock to take a more active hand in projects than might otherwise have been the case. It also sparked feelings of rivalry in Cutts, who made fun of the apprentice when his back was turned. Hitchcock repaid the condescension in later years, saying he had to save the day so often that he was "running even the director" of the pictures—a claim I no longer take at face value, since while

Hitchcock was surely an invaluable assistant, he clearly profited from observing the working methods and techniques of a seasoned mentor whose fortunes were on the rise.

All of the Cutts-Hitchcock movies were made on modest six-week schedules, and some were showcases for Betty Compson, a Hollywood star who came to England when Balcon, Freedman & Saville promised her a star-worthy salary of a thousand pounds a week. Hitchcock regarded the first of these, the 1923 romance *Woman to Woman*, as the first film he was fully involved in. "I was the general factotum," he recalled. "I wrote the script. I designed the sets, and I managed the production." It proved to be a first-rate calling card, welcomed as the "best American picture made in England" by the *Daily Express*, whose reviewer shared the common British opinion that Hollywood movies were more entertaining than their British counterparts.[2] After becoming a hit on English screens, *Woman to Woman* joined the rarified rank of British films earning high profits in the United States and also in Germany, where ill feelings from World War I had stifled earlier British exports.

Caught on the hop

Eager to keep the momentum going, the producers whisked *The White Shadow* into the works, and then rushed it to theaters with a marketing tag that was as unoriginal as it was uninspired: "The same Star, Producer, Author, Hero, Cameraman, Scenic Artist, Staff, Studio, Renting Company as *Woman to Woman*." Again the setting was Paris, and again the story was borrowed from Michael Morton, an author and playwright of the period. But this time box-office lightning failed to strike. "Engrossed in our first production, we had made no preparations for the second," Balcon conceded in his autobiography. "Caught on the hop, we rushed into production with a story called *The White Shadow*. It was as big a flop as *Woman to Woman* had been a success."[3]

Flop or no flop, *The White Shadow* allowed Hitchcock to continue his on-the-job training in an array of cinematic skills—scenario writing, set designing, film editing, and assisting the director whenever the need arose. It's hard to overstate the importance of his apprenticeship with Cutts, since the lessons he learned from working on silent movies continued to apply for the rest of his professional life. For him, the highest kind of cinema—the "pure cinema" that he valued above all else—was *visual* cinema that conveys narrative meaning, psychological depth, and emotional power through camerawork and editing alone. For vivid examples, remember the crop-dusting scene in *North by Northwest*, or the introduction of Jefferies at the beginning of *Rear Window*, or Marion's fatal shower and Norman's meticulous tidying in *Psycho*.

Reviewers found *The White Shadow* implausible and melodramatic. Hitchcock later scoffed at moviegoers who rated plausibility over momentum and suspense, but in this case, he must have known they had a valid point. A plot synopsis filed for copyright purposes is still extant, and untangling the complicated narrative is quite a task.

Critics applauded the production's performances and style, however, and here they were on solid ground. Outdoor scenes are gracefully composed and staged; a startling close-up of a feline sculpture introduces a bohemian café called the Cat Who Laughs, which then comes alive via spaciously composed views of a jazzy dive at its jazziest; a father-daughter misrecognition scene brings forth deep feelings with remarkable restraint. Memorable images abound: Compson's impish smile framed by a wreath of smoke and a jaunty hat; the varied group of men at a poker table she easily controls; Clive Brook's determined gaze accentuated by a streak of light across a dark background; and the delicate shading of an ivy-draped window enclosing a pensive face. Equally stirring is the artfully choreographed *movement* of these moving pictures as they flash upon the screen in a multifaceted rhythmic flow.

"Just as the sun casts a dark shadow, so does the soul throw its shadow of white, reflecting a purity that influences the lives of those upon whom the white shadow falls." So reads the opening text of *The White Shadow*, and while that's not exactly great poesy, it presages the spirited whites, somber darks, and intriguing shades of gray that conjoin to provide the film's striking look. Perhaps the rest of this florid romance will someday be unearthed and restored, but even the fragmentary version now available gives persuasive evidence of the creativity that was crystallizing in Hitchcock's imagination as he worked alongside the more seasoned, less inspired director who outranked him.

Gainsborough

Undaunted by the lamentable box-office fate of *The White Shadow*, plans went ahead at Balcon, Freedman & Saville for more pictures by Cutts and his gifted apprentice. *The Prude's Fall*, a 1925 release later known by the less regrettable title *Dangerous Virtue*, was summarily dismissed as "just a piece of film junk" by *Variety*, then as now the leading publication for entertainment news, reviews, and scuttlebutt. "New York's audience laughed at it and practically hooted it from the screen," the paper reported.[4] This was clearly an apt moment for Cutts and Hitchcock to seek a different production company, and events were trending in that direction for another reason as well. The aesthetics of *The White Shadow* had so irritated its British distributor—a well-known philistine named C.M. Woolf, who hated "artistic" movies—that he withdrew his backing from Balcon, Freedman & Saville, which soon went out of business. Balcon, the most energetic and prolific member of the troika, then founded Gainsborough Productions, which quickly put Cutts and Hitchcock onto its talent roster.

Their first enterprise under the new arrangement—and their third release of 1924, showing that Cutts's distractions didn't curtail their productivity—was *The Passionate Adventure*, a 1924 melodrama that attracted attention for its grand visual scale. "Some of the sets ... are unique," opined a writer for *Pictures and Picturegoer*, "especially the large hall which is seen so many times and from so many different angles.... Cutts tells me it was especially designed so as to give a minimum of two hundred different camera angles. The movie itself will doubtless be popular, for it is well acted, beautifully costumed and ably directed." Next came *The Blackguard*, known as *Die Prinzessin und der Geiger* at UFA, the German studio where the 1925 release was shot. *Variety* was pleased with the production, which is set during the Russian Revolution, and this critic too emphasized its impressive scale, saying the filmmakers had coupled "the German idea of realism ... with gigantic and, in some cases, almost unnatural settings. The result is … a picture which, whether it proves a showman's proposition [i.e., a moneymaker] or not, it is miles above the average production."[5]

Looking back on this period, it's clear that the poor financial performance of *The White Shadow* paradoxically boosted the careers of both Hitchcock and Balcon, since it pushed the latter toward establishing his own company—which became one of England's most respected, successful, and (yes) artistic production houses—and gave the former a knowledgeable, sympathetic, and shrewd producer who would soon facilitate his first film as a solo director, *The Pleasure Garden*, which Gainsborough co-produced. (It subsequently produced Hitchcock's inaugural suspense thriller, *The Lodger: A Story of the London Fog*, which Woolf, still waging war against artistic cinema, did his best to keep out of distribution. At first, Balcon didn't like it either, but Hitchcock and the art of film emerged triumphantly.)

Cutts also got past the financial failure of *The White Shadow* and remained a substantial fish in the medium-sized pond of British film. Hitchcock could have fared much worse in the senior-partner department, although nobody doubts that he would have mastered film technique and found his own distinctive voice under almost any circumstances. As critic Andrew Sarris observed, Hitchcock and cinema entered the world at almost the same moment and were made for each other from the start.

The directorial debut

Hitchcock made his directorial debut with *The Pleasure Garden*, a British-German co-production—the first of five joint efforts planned by Gainsborough Pictures and Emelka, a German studio not known for art films—and shot on Italian locations (Genoa, Lake Como) as well as Emelka stages. A lukewarm 1926 review in *The Observer* concisely summarized the plot, adapted by Eliot Stannard from the pseudonymous Oliver Sandys's popular novel: "Patsy [Virginia Valli] is a chorus girl and good. Jill [Carmelita Geraghty] is a country maid and terribly wicked. Jill joins the show, forsakes the swain to whom she swore to be true, runs through a succession of protectors, finally landing a prince and even a wedding-ring. Patsy marries the swain's friend, is deserted by him after a Como holiday, and, despite some misadventure, ends up with the swain himself."

The opening titles are hardly over when the aforementioned chorus line fills the screen—a bevy of high-spirited women, bare legs flashing below scanty costumes as they race down a spiral staircase and onto the stage of the Pleasure Garden Theatre, to be ogled by ladies and gentlemen whose refined appearance strikes an ironic contrast with the less-than-refined entertainment they've come to see. Motifs that would become longtime Hitchcock trademarks come immediately to the fore: voyeurism when the camera displays the dancers through the binoculars of a lascivious male spectator; female wiles when Patsy reveals brunette locks beneath her blonde hairpiece; feminine allure when the camera dwells on the showgirls undressing before bed; and crime when thieves purloin the money from Jill's purse.

These motifs are repeated, amplified, and joined to others as the film continues, showing Jill's rejection of her fiancé Hugh (John Stuart) in favor of a wealthy Russian prince (C. Falkenberg) and Patsy's marriage to a businessman named Levett (Miles Mander) whose deceptions bring her to Africa, leading to the story's climax. Although the film starts with the relatively modest crime of robbery, it escalates to murder in the African scenes, most brutally when Patsy's faithless husband drowns his African mistress because she's become inconvenient. Some critics have accused Hitchcock's films of wreaking disproportionate violence on women, but the situation is much subtler than such charges suggest—Levett's homicide, for instance, is seen as evil when it happens, and is punished by his own death when he attacks Patsy later on. Indeed, Hitchcock signals his sympathy with women in the very first scene, pointedly mocking the lecher who gawks at Patsy in the chorus line.

The most important assets of *The Pleasure Garden* are the confidence and expertise of its very young and talented director. One of its producers said it looked more like an American movie than a European one, but he shouldn't have been surprised, since Hitchcock willingly acknowledged the lessons he had learned from the many Americans in the British studios where he cut his directorial teeth. *The Pleasure Garden* was warmly received; a German trade paper called it "fresh and lively," and the somewhat hesitant *Observer* critic was nonetheless "eager and optimistic" about Hitchcock's future.

Hitchcock's second release, *The Mountain Eagle*, was his second and last Gainsborough-Emelka picture, shot at Emelka and in Tyrol in western Austria, where the Alps provided mountainous locations. This is the only completed Hitchcock film of which no copy is known to exist. A synopsis appeared in *The Bioscope* shortly after its London premiere in October 1926, and since there's little chance of ever seeing the movie, the summary is worth quoting:

> Beatrice Brent, school teacher in a small mountain village, incurs the enmity of Pettigrew, the local Justice of the Peace and owner of the village stores, because he believes that she encourages the attentions of his son Edward, a cripple.... Pettigrew, while questioning Beatrice, is himself influenced by her charm and attempts liberties which she strongly resents. He is so furious at the rebuff that he proclaims her as a wanton and she is driven from the village by the inhabitants. Beatrice is saved from their fury by a mysterious stranger known as Fearogod, who lives a solitary life in a cabin.... Fearogod takes Beatrice down to the village and compels Pettigrew to marry them.... Pettigrew, furious with rage, takes advantage of the fact that his son has left the village and arrests Fearogod for his murder.... Fearogod is kept in prison for over a year, when he decides to escape. He finds that his wife has a baby and he goes off with them to the mountains. When they find that the baby is taken ill, Fearogod goes back to the village for a doctor, where he sees old Pettigrew.... The sudden return of his son ... convinces the old man of the futility of proceeding with his accusations of murder, so he makes the best of matters by shaking hands with the man he persecuted and all is supposed to end happily.

You can't judge a movie by its synopsis, but when the British Film Institute says "it's unlikely that *The Mountain Eagle* is a lost masterpiece," one suspects the institute is correct. This despite its interesting cast, including Malcolm Keen, later seen in *The Lodger* and *The Manxman*, and Bernhard Goetzke, a star of Fritz Lang's expressionist fable *Destiny* (*Der Müde Tod*, 1921), as well as Hollywood actress Nita Naldi in one of her last films before the coming of talkies quenched her career.

Although it may never have reached British theaters, *The Mountain Eagle* played in Germany under its German title, *Der Bergadler*, and probably in the United States under its American title, *Fear o' God*, earning reviews that were so-so about the movie but respectful toward the young man behind the camera. "Hitchcock's direction is, as usual, thoroughly imaginative," declared *Kinematograph Weekly*, confident enough about the young man's talent to say "as usual" even though he had only one prior directing job to his credit. Then again, the paper added, "he has rather over-stressed the slow tempo" and indulged a story "too full of unconvincing twists." *The Bioscope* also belittled the story while praising the "skilful and at times brilliant direction."[6]

The most severe critic of *The Mountain Eagle* was Hitchcock himself. "It was a very bad movie," he told François Truffaut, blaming producers who forced Naldi on him in hopes of cracking the American market. "She had fingernails out to there," the director added. "Ridiculous!

The first "Hitchcock" film

The Lodger: A Story of the London Fog was adapted by screenwriter Eliot Stannard from a popular 1913 novel, *The Lodger,* by the prolific Marie Belloc Lowndes, known as Mrs. Belloc Lowndes to her many fans.[7] Blending suspense, melodrama, and occasional humor into an effectively entertaining package, if not a memorably Hitchcockian one, her story drew inspiration from the exploits of Jack the Ripper, the infamous East London murderer of the late 1880s; the subtitle was added by the filmmakers after Balcon settled on the book as the basis for Hitchcock's next project, feeling that the director's "strong sense of character and narrative could balance the mystery aspects of the story" and that the foggy nature of the narrative "would justify any eerie visual touches Hitchcock had learned from the Germans," as Donald Spoto writes in his Hitchcock biography."[8]

Hitchcock prepared for principal photography with an illustrator, sketching out every shot in every scene, noting the set designs, furnishings, and props, and essentially pre-planning the entire film, as he would continue to do throughout his career. Balcon recruited the fashionable actor, author, and songwriter Ivor Novello to play the title character, even though Novello insisted on a different ending from the one in Stannard's adaptation of Lowndes's story. In line with Hitchcock's love of ambiguity, Stannard left the Lodger's guilt or innocence for the viewer to decide; but Novello wanted a definitively "happy" ending in which his character's innocence is clear, and the studio supported the star. "They wouldn't let Novello even be considered as a villain," Hitchcock lamented. "The publicity angle carried the day."[9] To portray Daisy, the perky daughter of the tale, the producers hired June Tripp, who asked to be billed only by her first name.

Novello plays a dour young man who rents a room in the modest house of Mr. and Mrs. Bunting (Arthur Chesney and Marie Ault) at a time when London is being terrorized by a serial killer who preys on young blonde women. It so happens that the Buntings have a young blonde daughter, Daisy, and that her boyfriend Joe (Malcolm Keen) is a police detective trying to identify and capture the murderer before he strikes again. Taking note of the Lodger's mysterious origins and spooky demeanor, and spurred by jealousy over his proximity to Daisy, the love-struck Joe concludes that the newcomer himself may be the killer and steers his investigation accordingly, with results that take everyone by surprise.

Despite the director's painstaking preparations and meticulous work as the film was shot, the finished picture contained bits of unclear action that Cutts and Woolf used to support their contention—evidently motivated by ill feelings over Hitchcock's rapid rise and distaste for his "artistic" proclivities—that it should be relegated to the storeroom where *The Pleasure Garden* and *The Mountain Eagle* were still sitting, thanks to Woolf's final say on distribution and marketing. Balcon saved the day (and rescued Hitchcock's acutely endangered career) by bringing in Ivor Montagu, a young critic he had never met before, to watch the movie and offer a fresh assessment.

Montagu thought it was terrific, recommending only a few changes. On his advice, some mildly confusing scenes were done over, and—somewhat embarrassingly for Hitchcock, who had started as a title-card artist—the intertitles were cut down and given a new, cleverly symbolic design with a triangle motif. *The Lodger: A Story of the London Fog* premiered on February 14, 1927, and became a hit. "It is possible," the *Bioscope* declared, "that this film is the finest British production ever made."[10] Just as important, Spoto contends that this marked "the first time in British film history that the director received an even greater press than his stars."[11] Hitchcock's personal celebrity was off to a rousing start.

From The Ring to The Manxman

Hitchcock completed two more pictures in 1927, his busiest year as a director to date, although 1929 would be busier still. He took a rare screenwriting credit for *The Ring*, although Stannard and writer Walter C. Mycroft probably contributed to the scenario as well. The idea of a prizefighting film appealed to Hitchcock, who enjoyed spectator sports. For this production, he moved from Gainsborough to the newly formed British International Pictures, which was so pleased to have the rapidly rising filmmaker direct its first release that it offered him creative freedom and a salary making him the highest paid director in the land.[12]

The story juxtaposes the four corners of the boxing ring with the three corners of a love triangle. "One-Round" Jack Sanders (Carl Brisson) is a fairground fighter who promises to vanquish all comers in a single round. He's humiliated when a challenger beats him, but the loss doesn't seem too bad when the victorious pug turns out to be Bob Corby (Ian Hunter), the Australian champ. Their rivalry moves from the sports arena to the romantic arena when Bob takes a fancy to Jack's fiancée, the carnival snake-charmer Nelly (Lilian Hall-Davis), and hires Jack as a sparring partner as a way of being near her. Disappointed by the dull life Jack is giving her, Nelly grows close to Bob and finally runs away with him. Jack starts training for a revenge bout with high personal stakes, which ultimately occurs in London's staid old Albert Hall.

Hitchcock had fun playing with variations on the "ring" in the film's title, which signifies the boxing ring, the wedding ring slipped onto Nelly's finger—like handcuffs in some Hitchcock films, it suggests the confining aspects of romantic relationships—and a circular snake bracelet that Bob gives her as a secret love token. He also pushed the vulgarity envelope a bit, at one point showing a man hoisting his middle finger in a close-up. Charles Morgan of *The New York Times* praised Hitchcock for giving the film "a German variety of photographic angle and a German love of suggesting emotion very skilfully [sic] by means of circumstantial detail" as well as "an American smoothness and swiftness," while *Variety* called Brisson a "first-rate film actor with an engaging he-man personality and a strong flapper appeal."[13] Later critics have been enthusiastic as well. In terms of technique and formal symmetry, Jonathan Rosenbaum argues, *The Ring* is arguably the Hitchcock silent movie "worked out most conscientiously in strictly [cinematic] terms." Geoff Andrew of *Time Out* notes the "circular shape" of the story, Hitchcock's sharp eye for social detail, and his use of German expressionist methods to suggest psychological states, such as "a shot which 'melts' off the screen to evoke the cuckold's drunken slide into oblivion."[14] To this day, *The Ring* retains its hold on thoughtful viewers of silent cinema.

Novello returned to Hitchcock and Hitchcock returned to Gainsborough for his third 1927 release, *Downhill*, known to American audiences as *When Boys Leave Home*. In it Novello reprised his starring performance in the stage play *Down Hill*, which he and Constance Collier had written under the pseudonym David L'Estrange; he also reprised the fan-pleasing scene where his character cleans up after a rugby game, with bare legs in the play, a bare chest in the film. Stannard adapted the drama for the screen. In this version, Roddy Berwick (Novello) is expelled from school after reluctantly taking the blame for an offense committed by a friend, providing an early example of Hitchcock's transference-of-guilt motif. He then sinks into misery and ruin exacerbated by Julia Fotheringale (Isabel Jeans), his faithless lover and then wife, until a belated show of understanding from his father ushers in a last-minute happy ending. Although the director was less than fond of *Downhill*, its expressive lighting and communication of psychological states are praiseworthy.

Hitchcock shuttled back to BIP for *The Farmer's Wife*, his first picture of 1928. In addition to Stannard, no fewer than four uncredited writers (plus the director) labored to adapt the scenario from an enormously popular 1916 stage comedy. Looking at the lackluster result, one would never guess that such work had gone into it. The plot is a sub-fairy-tale trifle about a widowed gentleman farmer (Jameson Thomas) choosing a new spouse from the eligible ladies in the area, all of whom prove unsatisfactory when he starts courting them; in the end, he realizes that his modest housekeeper (Lillian Hall-Davis) is the ideal woman for him, as every half-awake member of the audience has been aware for the past hour or so. The movie's silliness aside, it contains Hitchcock's most muscular comedy scenes to date, often veering into full-throttle slapstick of a kind rarely found in his films. Its only other praiseworthy element is crisp cinematography by John J. Cox (sometimes billed as J.J. Cox or Jack Cox), who would shoot many other Hitchcock pictures in years to come.

Easy Virtue, produced by Gainsborough in 1928, is based on a 1926 play by the English polymath Noel Coward, whose talents embraced the full range of theatrical activity from writing, directing, and acting to singing, dancing, and composing.[15] Although he had written more than a dozen previous plays, *Easy Virtue* was one of several works that sealed his lofty reputation when it drew New York crowds in 1925 and London audiences a year later. Its language is expansive and assured, reflecting Coward's flair for sophisticated repartee, which naturally fell by the wayside in Hitchcock's silent movie. The plot survived, somewhat rejiggered by Stannard's adaptation but still cutting in its implied criticisms of the haut-bourgeois family and high society in general. Divorced by her husband after being falsely accused of adultery, Larita Filton (Isabel Jeans) becomes a pariah, stigmatized by her past despite the love of her second husband, John Whittaker (Robin Irvine), whose unsympathetic mother (Violet Farebrother) ultimately causes Larita's divorce from him as well. The film ends with one of the most memorable intertitles in Hitchcock's filmography. Leaving the court that has finalized her second divorce, clad in black and desperately sad, Larita faces a herd of scandal-hungry photographers and says, "Shoot! There's nothing left to kill." It's a haunting capstone to one of Hitchcock's best early pictures.

Hitchcock's third 1928 release, the BIP production *Champagne*, brought him back to romantic comedy after the strenuous farce of *The Farmer's Wife* and the decline-and-fall storylines of *Downhill* and *Easy Virtue*. The Girl (Betty Balfour) is a happy-go-lucky heiress who regards luxury and excitement as her everyday due. Deciding she needs a lesson in humility, her Father (Gordon Harker) pretends that losses in the stock market have abruptly obliterated his wealth—an unwitting omen of the 1929 crash, which inflicted that fate on thousands of actual investors—and that a modest, penny-pinching life will be their lot henceforth. The Girl takes a job at a nightclub, misunderstands the Boy (Jean Bradin) who wants to love and protect her, and gets involved with a mysterious Man (Theo Von Alten) whose motives appear to be ominous. As happens in many Hitchcock pictures, the happy ending is tempered with a suggestion of more conflict in the future. Although it's fairly light in tone, *Champagne* has similarities with *Easy Virtue* that bespeak Hitchcock's increasing ability to put his distinctive stamp on his films. Again he calls attention to the importance of vision in movies and in life, as when the first inventive shot in *Champagne*—cabaret partying seen through an upraised cocktail glass—recalls the view of a courtroom through a judge's monocle at the beginning of *Easy Virtue*. And again, the world of high society reveals a hidden side that is surprisingly dark.

The Manxman was Hitchcock's first 1929 release and his last picture to reach the screen exclusively as a silent film. It tells of an ill-starred loved triangle in a fishing village on the Isle of Man, doubled by Cornwall, where the film was shot. Pete Quilliam (Carl Brisson), a fisherman, wants to marry Kate Cregeen (Anny Ondra), and asks his lawyer friend Philip Christian (Malcolm Keen) to convey his honorable intentions to her father, Caesar (Randle Ayrton), an innkeeper. Caesar says no because Pete is poor, so Pete heads for Africa with hopes of striking it rich, asking Philip to keep an eye on Kate while he's away. Philip and Kate fall for each other, but then his aunt becomes the snob, insisting that marrying below his station will hurt his ambition of becoming a judge. Pete eventually returns, Kate marries him, and Philip gets to be a judge. But by now Kate is pregnant with Philip's child. Pangs of conscience, attempted suicide, and courtroom proceedings before judge Philip lead to the story's downbeat finale.

The scenario—the last of nine that Stannard wrote for Hitchcock—derives from an eponymous 1894 novel by the *Manxman* author, playwright, screenwriter, and critic Hall Caine, which George Loane Tucker had already turned into a popular film in 1916. Once again Hitchcock expressed disappointment with the result of his labor, even though it did nicely at the box office; the ending alone is so effectively somber and moody that the director's unhappiness seems misplaced. Noteworthy members of the principal cast include Keen, who had appeared in *The Mountain Eagle* and *The Lodger*, and Brisson, who had scored in *The Ring*. Ondra was a comic actress who achieved great success in Czechoslovakia and Germany before teaming with Hitchcock in *The Manxman*, and soon thereafter she signed on for the remarkable *Blackmail*, a major turning point for the director and the British cinema as a whole.

3

Talkies, Theatricality, and the Low Ebb

Like the recent *Downhill* and *Easy Virtue*, Hitchcock's next project, *Blackmail*, was based on a play, written this time by Charles Bennett, a young English actor and aspiring dramatist. Hitchcock saw its London production, starring the celebrated Tallulah Bankhead, in 1928. BIP chief executive John Maxwell bought the screen rights, and Hitchcock prepared the adaptation with neophyte scenarist Benn Levy, darkening the tone of the drama, which was pretty dark already. Principal photography commenced in February 1929 and editing was slated for two months later. But at that point, technological advances changed the course of film history.

Silent cinema started to acquire sound in the middle of the 1920s. A turning point arrived with the 1927 debut of Warner Bros.' musical drama *The Jazz Singer*, starring Al Jolson as a young Jew who would rather be an entertainer than follow family tradition and become a cantor. The studio took a considerable gamble by releasing a feature-length film with synchronized sound in a few scenes and a recorded music score throughout; it was far from clear that audiences would respond enthusiastically enough to recoup the film's $422,000 cost—almost double Warner Bros.' usual budget cap—and encourage exhibitors to invest in the new projectors and other paraphernalia needed to show talkies regularly, if indeed talkies caught hold in the industry.

Worries were needless. The movie was a hit and talkies were here to stay. The reverberations from this development were immediately heard across the pond, and where Hollywood had successfully ventured the British were sure to follow. In spring of 1929, Maxwell purchased a set of American sound-filming equipment—not the Vitaphone sound-on-disc device used for *The Jazz Singer* but the superior RCA Photophone sound-on-film system that was becoming an industry standard—and asked Hitchcock to change *Blackmail* from a silent picture to a talkie.

Photographs of people talking

Although it sounds counterintuitive today, Hitchcock was skeptical about the prospect of adding sound to movies. More precisely, he worried that sound would dilute cinema's unique status as the only art form that tells stories, conveys ideas, and expresses emotions by means of moving images alone. He summed up his position in his dialogue with Truffaut years later. Truffaut contended that film production "reached something near perfection" in the 1920s because the discipline of silent storytelling winnowed out "lesser talents"; introducing sound as a narrative crutch, Truffaut hypothesized, put that progress in jeopardy. "One might say," the French director concluded, "that mediocrity came back into its own with the advent of sound."

"I agree absolutely," Hitchcock responded. "In my opinion, that's true even today. In many of the films now being made, there is very little cinema: they are mostly what I call 'photographs of people talking.' When we tell a story in cinema, we should resort to dialogue only when it's impossible to do otherwise. I always try first to tell a story in the cinematic way, through a succession of shots and bits of film in between." Since dialogue is essentially theatrical, he continued, movies stop being a truly distinctive medium when spoken words are added. "In writing a screenplay," Hitchcock declared, "it is essential to separate clearly the dialogue from the visual elements and whenever possible, to rely more on the visual than the dialogue."[1]

Hitchcock's strong views notwithstanding, the industry went through a major metamorphosis in the late 1920s, and he had no choice but to participate. Beyond this, he loved to take on challenges and experiment with new techniques, and the arrival of sound was an opportunity to do both. In the end, he completed two versions of *Blackmail*—a sound version for properly equipped first-run theaters and a silent version (released a little later) for theaters that hadn't yet made the upgrade.

The big question, of course, is whether Hitchcock managed to stick by his principles and use sound in creative, nonredundant, and untheatrical ways. The answer is a resounding yes. The first talkie from a British studio is positively ingenious in its use of sound.

Blackmail

The origin of *Blackmail* as a silent project is evident at the beginning, when officers from Scotland Yard track down and capture a criminal who plays no further part in the story; here the silent and sound versions are identical except for the latter version's music track. Dialogue kicks in when the main body of the story begins, but some of the most riveting episodes still contain few spoken words.

The protagonist is Alice White (Anny Ondra), the flirtatious daughter of a London shopkeeper. Out with her detective boyfriend, Frank Webber (John Longden), she picks a few squabbles with him and then slips away to meet another man, an artist named Crewe (Cyril Ritchard), whom she evidently doesn't know very well. Crewe entices her to visit his studio on the top floor of a residential building, and offers to paint her picture if she puts on a cute little costume. When she complies, Crewe's seduction escalates into a full-out assault behind the curtains of his bed. Alice escapes by stabbing him with a knife on a bedside table.

Severely traumatized, Alice makes her way home and pretends that she was asleep in her bedroom all night. The neighborhood soon hears about the "murder," and Alice barely maintains her composure when discussion turns that way at the breakfast table and in her father's shop. Investigating the crime, Frank finds a clue that points to Alice as the perpetrator. He decides to protect her guilty secret, but his effort is shaken by the appearance of Tracy (Donald Calthrop), a sleazy blackmailer. Frank finds a way to pin the killing on Tracy, who leaps through a window and winds up in the British Museum, where his doom is quickly sealed. Meanwhile, Alice's tormented conscience convinces her to give herself up at Scotland Yard, but Frank arrives in time to stop her from confessing. She tells him the extenuating circumstances of the killing, and they leave at peace with each other.

But it's clear that Alice won't be at peace with her conscience for a long time to come.

An unforeseen challenge of early sound cinema, when post-dubbing techniques were not yet available, was sorting out the voices of actors whose vocal tones or accents were irrelevant in silent films but now mattered a great deal. Hitchcock hired Ondra to play Alice when he started *Blackmail* as a silent film, and when it became a talkie an awkward problem loomed: why would a London shopkeeper's daughter have a noticeable Czech accent? To solve this without scrapping footage already filmed, Hitchcock had the English actress Joan Barry stand outside camera range and speak Alice's lines while Ondra lip-synched the dialogue. It's a simple trick, and it works; few viewers notice Ondra's slight hesitations and adjustments unless they know about the off-screen setup in advance.

That aside, many moments in this groundbreaking film manifest Hitchcock's creativity with sound. One of the best is the scene where Alice is breakfasting with her parents on the morning after the killing. Nobody connects her with the crime, although she is still so traumatized that she can barely function. A gabby neighbor drops in and fills the air with lurid gossip about the event, taking umbrage at the idea of killing a man with a knife instead of some more genteel instrument. A close-up of Alice's face fills the screen as she listens, and the neighbor's words quickly become gobbledygook in which only one word—"knife"—comes through clearly and repeatedly, stabbing Alice's agonized mind until she tries to cut a piece of bread for her father and almost breaks down in front of everyone. Immediately after the killing, we saw Alice's surroundings—streets and sidewalks full of ghostly figures and uncanny portents—as she perceived them through a fog of psychological shock, and now we hear the neighbor's voice through a disorienting haze of troubled consciousness. Hitchcock sacrifices verbal clarity in order to create the aural equivalent of a point-of-view camera perspective, an amazingly bold move at a time when audiences were still absorbing the novelty of sound cinema.[2]

Blackmail builds on techniques Hitchcock had developed in previous films and points to ideas he would explore in films to come. Instances abound: his characteristic humor glows when a shadow on Crewe's face recalls the mustachio of an old-fashioned melodrama villain; the caged bird in Alice's bedroom is a touch of personal symbolism; a key visual trope—a painting of a laughing jester, first seen in Crewe's studio—reappears in multiple scenes with different emotional overtones each time, exemplifying Hitchcock's mastery of the Kuleshov effect discussed earlier. Laughter also occurs on the soundtrack, most notably in the final scene, when the jester painting makes its last appearance as Frank and another cop chortle over a silly joke at Alice's expense. Once again male primacy asserts itself, flippantly echoing the sexist arrogance that was interrupted when Alice killed Crewe in self-defense but continues in other ways throughout male-dominated society. Tania Modleski gets this exactly right in the inspired title of her feminist take on this extraordinary film: "Rape vs Mans/laughter."[3]

Hitchcock's next picture does not deserve similar kudos. *Juno and the Paycock*, based on a 1924 drama by the celebrated Irish playwright Sean O'Casey, is a rote exercise in filmed theater. Released to US theaters as *The Shame of Mary Boyle*, it unfolds almost entirely in the dilapidated tenement home of Captain Boyle (Edward Chapman), a ne'er-do-well who was never actually a captain, and Juno (Sara Allgood), his long-suffering wife; other characters include their daughter Mary (Kathleen O'Regan), who's being courted by a worker and a lawyer, and their son Johnny (John Laurie), who lost an arm fighting for Irish independence. The title refers to Juno's nickname for her self-important peacock of a husband, and the story is propelled by the false hopes and misguided actions of the family when they are wrongly informed that an inheritance is coming their way.

O'Casey cycles through familiar motifs of 20th-century Irish drama—alcoholic men, discontented women, the violence of low-grade civil war, the suspicions bred by informers and cheats—and invests them with considerable warmth and intensity. Hitchcock sticks largely to the original script, which he regarded as excellent in its story, mood, characters, and blend of wit and tragedy. Yet he fails to build much narrative momentum, occasional interludes of suspense and comedy notwithstanding. "I could see no way of narrating [the play] in cinematic form," he confessed later. "I photographed the play as imaginatively as possible," he added, "but from a creative viewpoint it was not a pleasant experience." Critics loved it despite all. "I had the feeling I was dishonest, that I had stolen something," Hitchcock said of the enthusiastic reviews.[4] Time has proven the director right—it is a thoroughly uninspired film—and the critics wrong.

Murder!

Not surprisingly, Hitchcock rebounded almost immediately. His emphatically titled 1930 thriller *Murder!* is based on a breezily entertaining 1928 novel called *Enter Sir John*, coauthored by Clemence Dane and the same Helen Simpson who would write dialogue for *Sabotage* and inspire *Under Capricorn* in later years.[5] Hitchcock also directed a German-language version of the film, which was not an uncommon practice in the days before subtitles and post-dubbing; titled *Mary* and released in 1931, it's a slightly streamlined replay with few significant differences.

The hero of *Murder!* is Sir John Menier (Herbert Marshall), an actor and manager of a theater company. Summoned for jury duty, he deliberates the case of Diana Baring (coincidentally played by Norah Baring), an actress charged with homicide after being found with the corpse of a rival actress who has been bludgeoned to death with a poker. The evidence against Diana seems strong—she was found in a traumatized state, like Alice in *Blackmail*, wearing clothes stained with blood—and most jurors consider her either guilty of cold-blooded murder or so perilously deranged that leaving her at large would be a danger to society.

Sir John once knew Diana and feels she must be innocent, but the others badger him into voting for conviction. Nagged by his conscience the next day, he vows to investigate the case with an eye to exonerating the young woman. Drawing on his life experience and theatrical expertise, he sets to work with the assistance of stage manager Ted Markham (Edward Chapman) and Markham's wife Doucie (Phyllis Konstam), eventually concluding that the killer was Handel Fane (Esme Percy), a male actor of mixed ethnicity (a "half-caste," in the language of the novel and film) who specializes in female roles. Sir John jangles Fane's nerves by confronting him with a theatrical script that describes the actual crime—rather like "The Mousetrap," the incriminating play cooked up by Hamlet in Shakespeare's tragedy—and soon afterward Fane commits suicide during a trapeze performance, while Sir John sits in the audience. A happy ending thus arrives for everyone except Fane and his unfortunate victim.

Murder! is no less inventive than *Blackmail* in its uses of sound. When the jury members browbeat Sir John, for instance, Hitchcock edits the voices and images into a stylized cascade of escalating tension. Instead of cutting to the courtroom when Diana receives her death sentence, Hitchcock puts the judge's words on the soundtrack while keeping the camera in the jury room, now empty of everyone except a clerk straightening things up. To convey Sir John's ruminations while he shaves and listens to music the morning after the trial, Hitchcock arranged an interior monologue—a groundbreaking technique in 1930, when sound and picture had to be captured simultaneously—by playing Marshall's voice from a hidden wire recorder while a symphony orchestra played "radio" music just outside camera range. Once again Hitchcock demonstrated his flair for getting maximum benefit from cutting-edge film technology.

"This low ebb of my career"

Not even a brilliant filmmaker like Hitchcock could be expected to turn out an eternal stream of masterpieces, and after *Murder!* he went into a slump that he recognized as his all-time creative nadir. It began with his 1931 film *The Skin Game*, another venture in filmed theater. The source was a wordy but engrossing 1920 play by John Galsworthy that had already reached the screen in a 1921 adaptation directed by B.E. Doxat-Pratt and starring Edmund Gwenn, who reprised his portrayal of Mr. Hornblower in Hitchcock's version.[6] The plot revolves around rivalry between the well-to-do Hillcrest family and the up-and-coming Hornblower family; the heads of both households (Gwenn and C.V. France) are shamelessly fixated on their own interests, but the old-money clan precipitates a crisis by exploiting a secret about the nouveau-riche clan—the fact that Hornblower's daughter-in-law, Chloe (Phyllis Konstam), used to earn her living by posing as a mistress in divorce cases.

Responsibility for the film's overall dullness rests partly with

Galsworthy, whose agreement with BIP ruled out changes to his script. The rest of the blame goes to Hitchcock, who filmed the drama with four cameras (so the dialogue wouldn't be disrupted in the editing process) but still failed to give it visual life. His long-take strategy makes for awkward staging at times, relegating a speaking character to off-screen space when dramatic logic calls for the person to be visible, and no Hitchcock film has drearier lighting. "Mr. Hitchcock's imagination is never particularly keen during this production," the *New York Times* opined, "and frequently there are lengthy discourses between two characters without the slightest semblance of movement to the picture."[7] Hitchcock basically agreed: "I didn't make it by choice," he remarked, "and there isn't much to be said about it."[8]

There is at least a little to be said about it, though, and the news is not all bad. Hitchcock came up with some noteworthy shot framings, as when we hear an argument through an open doorway while the camera (recalling the scene in *Murder!* with the empty jury room) shows a chauffeur killing time outside. A suspenseful auction scene gets additional energy from a jittery camera that surveys the room with nervous, jumpy movements, whipping toward sudden bits of action so quickly that the image blurs. These clever moments can almost earn forgiveness for the picture's many flaws. Almost.

Fred and Emily = Alfred and Alma

Many connoisseurs find that the 1931 comedy-thriller *Rich and Strange* is indeed rich and strange, if not a remarkable work on the order of *Blackmail* or *Murder!* It also appears to be one of Hitchcock's most candidly semi-autobiographical films. Although it's based on a 1930 novel by the Australian writer Dale Collins, the director said its real inspiration was his honeymoon—an excursion to St. Moritz, Switzerland, in 1927—and he took one of his rare writing credits here. Sure enough, when you hear the main character's names, Fred and Emily Hill, it's easy to think of Alfred and Alma Hitchcock.

Although the film was called *East of Shanghai* in US markets, the title *Rich and Strange* is itself slightly strange, striking a Shakespearean note that portends little about the movie to come. Its source is Ariel's mysterious song in act 1, scene 2 of *The Tempest*:

Full fathom five thy father lies.
Of his bones are coral made.
Those are pearls that were his eyes.
Nothing of him that doth fade
But doth suffer a sea change
Into something rich and strange.
Sea nymphs hourly ring his knell.
   Burden, within: Ding dong.
Hark, now I hear them: ding dong bell.[9]

The film tells a peripatetic tale. Bored with their run-of-the-mill married life, Fred (Henry Kendall) and Emily (Joan Barry) seek recreation and refreshment by signing up for a world cruise. Complications ensue when Emily cozies up to Commander Gordon (Percy Marmont), a fellow passenger, and more trouble comes when Fred becomes infatuated with a Princess (Betty Amann) who may not be what she seems. After traveling to Paris, Singapore, Port Said, and elsewhere, Fred and Emily head for home on a shabby steamer, their money and patience exhausted. The boat suffers a spectacular crash, ending their vacation and almost ending their lives, but they finally make it back to London, where they're still quarreling when the final scene fades out.

Rich and Strange benefits from scrappy performances by Barry—all of her, not just her voice as in *Blackmail*—and Marmont, who made two more Hitchcock films in the 1930s. The cinematographers, John Cox and Charles Martin, ably captured the general feel of the story's varied settings, all filmed at the BIP studio. The picture's experimental blend of sound and silent-movie devices (title cards, numerous scenes without dialogue) proved too strange for audiences and critics in 1931. In later years, however, it acquired a cult following thanks to the same experimental qualities that originally dampened its commercial prospects.

Preposterous details, Viennese melodies

Filmed before *Rich and Strange* but released several months later, *Number Seventeen* had a similar fate when it was new and fared worse in subsequent years, largely failing to persuade even cultists that something like entertainment value lies beneath its silly surfaces. Based on a play by J. Jefferson Farjeon, the allegedly suspenseful plot involves a group of criminals hiding after a robbery in a deserted house above a railroad depot, waiting for a train that will take them to safety; in these spooky surroundings Detective Barton (John Stuart), posing under the name Fordyce, gets the goods on the gang with help from hobo Ben (Leon M. Lion) and deaf-mute Nora Brant (Anne Grey).

Hitchcock regarded the play as a compendium of clichés, and when BIP insisted that he direct it, he decided to spoof it instead of playing it straight. A crime thriller had to culminate with a chase, so according to Rodney Ackland, who penned the movie with Hitchcock and Reville, they dreamed up an over-the-top chase with "details so preposterous that excitement would give way to gales of laughter," and then wrote the whole screenplay with that spirit in mind.[10] The chase is certainly kinetic, but overall the film is most famous for its incomprehensible story. Hitchcock wreaked his revenge on Farjeon's play, but it rebounded on BIP and on himself. His relationship with the studio had been increasingly strained, and this was their last picture together.

Edmund Gwenn returned, this time as Johann Strauss the Elder, in *Waltzes from Vienna*, a musical biopic filmed in 1933 and released in US theaters as *Strauss' Great Waltz*. Esmond Knight plays Johann Strauss the Younger, while Fay Compton plays wealthy Countess Helga von Stahl and Jessie Matthews, the film's nominal star, portrays Therese "Rasi" Ebeseder, the nice girl of the story. A brief British Film Institute synopsis gives the gist: "Young Johann 'Schani' Strauss is torn between two women and two career choices—bakery or music—and his arrogant composer father is no help: he thinks Schani's new 'Blue Danube' waltz has no musical merit. Will it ever get performed?" This is Hitchcock's most musical film to date, taking advantage of the industry's greatly improved techniques for sound recording, editing, and dubbing. It is also the only musical he ever made, although music plays a key role in other films, including the one he made next.[11]

Its tunefulness notwithstanding, Hitchcock regarded *Waltzes from Vienna* as another lost opportunity on the order of *Rich and Strange* and *Number Seventeen.* Fortunately, it proved to be the last stop on his journey through the doldrums. "To all appearances," he told Truffaut, "I seemed to have gone into a creative decline in 1933 when I made *Waltzes from Vienna,* which was very bad. And yet the talent must have been there all along since I had already conceived the project for *The Man Who Knew Too Much,* the picture that re-established my creative prestige."[12] It certainly did.

4

The Classic Thriller Sextet

T he all-important period from 1934 to 1938 brought a string of six consecutive films that restored Hitchcock's reputation, fortified his status in the industry, and definitively affirmed his special talent for crafting high-octane suspense pictures laced with humor and romance. The pictures came to be called the classic thriller sextet, and at least three of them—*The Man Who Knew Too Much* (1934), *The Thirty-Nine Steps* (1935), and *The Lady Vanishes* (1938)—are popular classics to this day.[1]

Now working for the Gaumont British Picture Corporation at a time when Britain's film industry was in a healthy and productive state, Hitchcock benefited from the availability of stars and the skills of such able collaborators as Gaumont British production chief Michael Balcon, now a top figure in British cinema and producer of two films in the sextet; Charles Bennett, who contributed to all but one of the sextet's screenplays; Ivor Montagu, the associate producer of all but two; Bernard Knowles, who photographed four; Oscar Werndorff, the art director for three; and of course Alma Reville, who supervised the script continuity for each production.

It's hard to overstate Hitchcock's high value for the studio, where "Hitchcock films" became a discrete production category, a level sometimes reached by stars but hardly ever by directors. By the middle of the decade, Hitchcock was regarded "as a kind of genre in himself," in film historian Tom Ryall's words, "firmly established in terms of directorial identity in contrast to his career at BIP which may fairly be described as meandering."[2] The movie that launched these happy developments was *The Man Who Knew Too Much*, a kinetic entertainment scripted by five writers but bearing Hitchcock's signature in every frame. *The Lodger* may have been the first true Hitchcock film, but *The Man Who Knew Too Much* has been called "the first one-hundred-percent Hitchcock picture."[3]

Incongruous crime

As with the less fortunate *Rich and Strange*, the idea behind *The Man Who Knew Too Much* may have originated with the Hitchcock honeymoon in the Swiss resort of St. Moritz, the kind of decent, rock-solid environment that the director loved to afflict with incongruous crime and chaos. The story centers on the Lawrence family: Jill (Edna Best), a prize-winning skeet shooter; Bob (Leslie Banks), her husband; and Betty (Nova Pilbeam), their frisky daughter. The review in *Variety* summarizes the plot in that publication's usual snappy manner:

> Starts at a party in St Moritz. A man is shot during a dance. He whispers to a friend [she has just met] that there's a message in a brush in his bathroom. Friend realizes the dying man was in the secret service and gets the message. Before he can communicate with the police, he is handed a note saying his daughter has been kidnapped and will be killed if he talks.
>
> Back to London and the cops can't make the man or his wife say anything. Finally, the man locates the gang's meeting place. He discovers that an attempt will be made to kill a famous international statesman at the Albert Hall that night and manages to communicate that news to his wife, although he is held prisoner.[4]

High points include a fight that Bob wins by knocking out a dentist with his own laughing gas, and a visit Bob pays, along with his sidekick Clive, to the curious Tabernacle of the Rising Sun, where Clive gets hypnotized while Bob finds a clue to Betty's whereabouts and the site of the planned assassination.

The most ingeniously constructed scene is the climax at the Albert Hall, a venerable London institution that dates from Victorian times and is, therefore, another ideal place for Hitchcock to discombobulate with evil doings. Here the evildoers intend to kill a foreign diplomat during a concert, firing a fatal shot at the precise moment when crashing cymbals will drown out the sound. Bob is nearby with Betty, hearing the concert on a radio, but Jill is in the auditorium, only now fully grasping the situation. She thwarts the assassins with a scream, and everyone ends up in a massive shootout that ends the picture.

New York Times reviewer Andre Sennwald found the film's lighting and photography "inferior according to Hollywood standards," but praised it nonetheless as "the swiftest screen melodrama this column can recall," unfolded by Hitchcock in "brief and tantalizing scenes which merge so breathlessly that you are always rapt and tense." He was also thrilled by Peter Lorre, who "is able to crowd his rôle [as Abbott, one of the killers] with dark and terrifying emotions without disturbing his placid moon face."[5] Lorre was a Jew who fled Hitler's Germany soon after electrifying moviegoers with his portrayal of a child murderer in Fritz Lang's extraordinary *M* (1931), and although he would eventually settle in Hollywood, his work for Hitchcock in this film and *Secret Agent* is excellent. *The Man Who Knew Too Much* is somewhat diminished by Pilbeam's overeager acting and by the overkill of the climactic gun battle, which runs out of inspiration before it runs out of bullets. Its value as a turning point for Hitchcock is indisputable, however.

Nothing whatever diminishes *The 39 Steps*, the second entry in the sextet, based on a 1915 novel by John Buchan that reads like a preliminary sketch for the action-filled yet psychologically resonant drama that Hitchcock made from it.[6] The book's hero is Richard Hannay, a well-liked protagonist who figured prominently in four more Buchan novels between 1916 and 1936 and appeared briefly in two others. The movie commences in a London music hall where the act of an entertainer called Mr. Memory (Wylie Watson) is disrupted by gunfire. Hannay (Robert Donat) is present, and in the ensuing confusion he meets a woman named Annabella Smith (Lucie Mannheim), takes her back to his flat, and learns that she is a British agent urgently trying to prevent an espionage ring—led by a nefarious man known to have a damaged finger on one hand—from spiriting military secrets out of the country. When she is murdered that night in Hannay's home, making him an automatic suspect for the police, he goes on the lam, following a Scottish map on which Annabella has marked a destination. In the course of his adventures, he finds—but fails to capture—the spy, gets handcuffed to a woman named Pamela (Madeleine Carroll) who has been trying to turn him in, and ultimately cracks the case and gets the girl. The film ends at the music hall where everything began.

In some ways, *The 39 Steps* is a logical follow-up to *The Man Who Knew Too Much*, using a few of its basic elements in new ways. Again secret agents have awful plans, the death of an enigmatic stranger plunges good people into danger, and the climax happens in a cultural venue, although this time it's not the high-class Albert Hall but the toney London Palladium vaudeville house. Equally important are elements that recur in future films, becoming reliable Hitchcock trademarks: a hero on the run from cops and crooks alike, a couple who start as adversaries but bond when circumstances chain them together, and a MacGuffin that's irrelevant to the audience—we don't care *what* the top-secret information is—but does a great job of making the characters race entertainingly around. The best scenes in *The 39 Steps* have terrific emotional power as well, most notably when Hannay spends a night with an unfeeling Scottish crofter (John Laurie) and his mistreated wife (Peggy Ashcroft), getting a glimpse of domestic misery that lends unforgettable poignancy to the film.

The titles of *Secret Agent* and *Sabotage* have given rise to considerable confusion over the years. *Sabotage* is a loose adaption of Joseph Conrad's 1907 novel *The Secret Agent: A Simple Tale*, about a plot to bomb the Royal Observatory in Greenwich, England, set in motion by an agent provocateur of a foreign power who hopes to spur the British authorities toward more belligerent action against the forces of anarchy and terror.[7] The film titled *Secret Agent*, on the other hand, has nothing to do with Conrad's novel; it is adapted very loosely from the 1928 book *Ashenden or: The British Agent* by W. Somerset Maugham, who had briefly been a secret agent himself.[8] *The Secret Agent* premiered in May 1936 and *Sabotage* at the end of the same year.

Ashenden qualifies as a short-story collection in some respects and a novel in others, since it contains a number of stand-alone chapters as well as connected chapters that develop sustained storylines. Some adventures of the eponymous hero, a writer, are based on Maugham's own experiences as an operative based in Switzerland and dispatched to Russia with instructions to help the Provisional Government stave off the Bolshevik threat, a mission that obviously failed. "Ashenden was depressed," Maugham wrote drily in the final chapter, "because all his careful schemes had come to nothing."[9]

The tasks have a better outcome in Hitchcock's film *Secret Agent*, which takes its cue from two of Maugham's chapters, "The Hairless Mexican" and "The Traitor," and from a stage adaptation by Campbell Dixon that fills out the romantic angle. Bennett's screenplay reshuffled a few of Maugham's motifs—coded messages, Swiss locations, a mountain-climbing excursion, a train journey, a spymaster known as R, a character called the Hairless Mexican, a wife with an absent husband—into a narrative bearing only fleeting resemblances to the book. John Gielgud plays the pseudonymous Ashenden, partnered with Madeleine Carroll as Elsa Carrington, the sham "wife" assigned to work with him. Also present are Robert Young as Robert Marvin, a flirtatious American who is not what he seems, and Peter Lorre as the Hairless Mexican, so called by his ironic superiors because he is not Mexican and has lots of hair.

Playing up the humor for which his thrillers were increasingly known, Hitchcock took the unusual step of pairing Gielgud with Lorre in long stretches of the story, making the former a sort of high-toned Bud Abbott to the latter's outlandish Lou Costello, until a dark twist at the climax sunders them for good. And again, Hitchcock inserted effective touches that echo or anticipate other films. The chase through the chocolate factory, for instance, recalls the pursuit through the British Museum in *Blackmail*, using expressive camera angles to show the relationships between characters and their surroundings. And a remarkable moment of sound-image disjunction—when a man's fall to his death is accompanied by the wail of his grieving dog—recalls the juxtaposition of a woman's visible scream and a train's audible whistle in *The 39 Steps*.

Sabotage, also scripted by Bennett, took similar liberties with Conrad's great novel. The shopkeeper becomes a movie-theater owner; mentally disabled Stevie turns into a bright youngster; instead of committing suicide at the end, the heroine walks off with a handsome detective; and the anarchists and operatives are now vaguely defined subversives whose hazy agenda is a MacGuffin par excellence. The film isn't Conrad, but it works well enough on its own terms.

The movie begins with an on-screen audience leaving the Bijou Theater, where the show has abruptly stopped because of a widespread power outage caused by—you guessed it—sabotage. The modest movie house is owned by Carl Anton Verloc (Oscar Homolka) and his wife Sylvia (Sylvia Sidney), who live in the back. The third member of the household is Sylvia's little brother Stevie (Desmond Tester), who joined her when she emigrated from America in a vain effort to dodge the ravages of the Great Depression. Sylvia knows her husband is a letdown in the marriage department, but she doesn't know he works for a ring of foreign agents who are wreaking havoc in England, pulling off disruptions like the power-station bombing as a smokescreen for their larger operations abroad. Someone who does know this is Ted Spencer (John Loder), a detective keeping tabs on Carl while posing as the assistant to a nearby grocer.

Carl's power-station sabotage was something of a fizzle, so his next assignment is much more lethal. Meeting his contact in an aquarium, he receives instructions to place a bomb in the heart of Piccadilly Circus, where it is timed to explode at 1:45 in the afternoon. Carl has caught on to Ted's surveillance, so he gives Stevie the delivery job—the bomb is hidden in a 35mm film-can package, and Stevie knows nothing of its nature—with strict instructions to leave it at the designated location by 1:30 at the latest. Stevie being a kid, and London being a crowded and bustling city, the boy misses the deadline and gets blown up on a bus. Soon thereafter Carl meets his doom at Sylvia's hands.

Hitchcock never forgave himself for the manner of Stevie's demise. The boy is an innocent and sympathetic character, and the sequence is superbly constructed for suspense, but the payoff is the opposite of what audiences want, as the director belatedly realized. The film has some remarkably vivid moments, though—the aquarium rendezvous set off with uncanny sea creatures, Stevie's halting progress during his fatal errand, and especially the scene near the end when traumatized Sylvia gazes at the Walt Disney cartoon *Who Killed Cock Robin?* (1935) in the Bijou, its death-laden imagery touching deep chords of misery in her while the audience unknowingly laughs. Hitchcock trademarks are present too, such as the traumatized heroine killing a man while virtually in a trance. *Sabotage* fared very well with critics, allowing Hitchcock and Gaumont British to end their association—the company was giving up production to focus entirely on distribution—on cordial terms. Hitchcock returned to Gainsborough for his last two British films.

Young and Innocent, released in US theaters as *The Girl Was Young*, is a variation on the *39 Steps* theme—a man running from the police while he tries to clear his name with reluctant help from a woman he hardly knows. Here he is Robert Tisdall (Derrick de Marney), a writer, and he's in big trouble when his actress friend Christine Clay (Pamela Carme) is murdered, evidently strangled with the belt from Robert's raincoat. His future looks grim, and it looks even grimmer when the police learn he is a big beneficiary of Christine's will. His lawyer, Briggs (J.H. Roberts), has no real interest in defending him when he's arrested, but he manages to escape from the courthouse and hook up with Erica Burgoyne (Nova Pilbeam), who happens to be the daughter of the chief constable (Percy Marmont), and they go on the hunt for the real killer. The ensuing chase brings them to an abandoned mill, an old mine shaft, and finally, a swanky hotel ballroom where they find their quarry, Guy (George Curzon), a man identifiable by his twitchy eyes. Secondary characters include Erica's Aunt Margaret (Mary Clare) and uncle Basil (Basil Radford), as well as a helpful tramp known as Old Will (Edward Rigby).

Hitchcock deploys humor more consistently and successfully here than in *Secret Agent* a year earlier, anticipating the artful balance of lightness and darkness in *The Lady Vanishes* a year later. And the film climaxes with one of the most bravura cinematic strokes in any early Hitchcock film. We know the evildoer is in the dance hall (another musical milieu for a Hitchcock climax) but we don't know who he is until the camera swoops purposefully over the dancers, heads in the direction of the band, and closes in on the drummer with the relentlessness of fate, framing him in a tight close-up just as the telltale twitch convulses his face, establishing him as the killer in the literal blink of an eye. He is wearing blackface makeup, less offensive to audiences (white ones, at least) in 1937 than today, but the maquillage can't disguise his nervous tic, a visible metaphor for the wayward temperament that made him a murderer. Although *Young and Innocent* is not among Hitchcock's finest pictures, he weaves invocations of vision and evocations of theatricality, artifice, and disguise into its fabric with subtlety, dexterity, and confidence.

The classic thriller sextet concluded with *The Lady Vanishes*, which stands with *The 39 Steps* atop the list of Hitchcock's best British films. Its source was *The Wheel Spins*, a 1936 novel by Ethel Lina White, then one of Britain's most popular crime-fiction authors. More important, it was scripted for Gainsborough by Sidney Gilliat and Frank Launder, a triple-threat team who wrote (and sometimes produced and/or directed, together or individually) more than two dozen films between 1936 and 1966. Among them are thrillers (Gilliat's *Green for Danger*, 1946) and comedies (Launder's *The Belles of St. Trinian's*, 1954), many of them, especially in the 1940s, with a Hitchcockian eye for ordinary people in unusual circumstances.[10] *The Lady Vanishes* is the duo's most celebrated legacy, thanks to their own talents and to the good fortune that put their screenplay into the hands of a director ideally suited to its mingling of excitement and wit.

The story begins in a Central European country called Bandrika, where numerous travelers are temporarily stranded in a hotel because an avalanche has immobilized their train. One is Gilbert Redman (Michael Redgrave), who enters the film tootling on a clarinet, and another is Iris Henderson (Margaret Lockwood), whose sleep is disrupted by the woodwind sounds emanating from the room overhead. While complaining about the noise, she meets the matronly Miss Froy (Dame May Whitty), a governess destined to be a central figure in the intrigues to come. Music pipes up again when a man serenades Miss Froy outside her window, and the film becomes emphatically Hitchcockian when the performer below is strangled to death.

Back on the train when the rails are clear, Miss Froy socializes a bit with Iris and then vanishes. Nobody knows where she is, or remembers seeing her, and if any passengers *have* seen her, they won't admit it. Iris looks for her high and low, interacting with a motley bunch of fellow travelers including Dr. Egon Hartz (Paul Lukas), a brain specialist; the Baroness (Mary Clare), wife of a propaganda official; The Great Doppo (Philip Leaver) and Signora Doppo (Zelma Vas Dias), an Italian magician and his spouse; Eric Todhunter (Cecil Parker) and "Mrs. Todhunter" (Linden Travers), secretive adulterers; and Charters (Basil Radford) and Caldicott (Naunton Wayne), cricket fanatics en route to a match. When Iris gets conked on the head by a falling flowerpot, even she starts to doubt whether the dowager really existed. Then an unexpected clue confirms the old lady's reality beyond a shadow of a doubt, putting Iris and Gilbert on track to resolve the mysteries surrounding her disappearance.

Trains have an inherent visual tension: they offer space for movement and action, yet they're claustrophobically constricted with their narrow corridors, small compartments, and lack of egress between stations. Hitchcock takes full advantage of this in *The Lady Vanishes*, and he also stocks his train with semi-surreal images, such as a body shrouded in bandages, a trunk with a secret exit, and a nun decked out in high-heeled shoes, And he wraps the novelty of these touches into a reassuringly Hitchcockian package, complete with an exemplary MacGuffin—a vital national secret that matters to the characters but not to us—and a man and woman made into a couple by circumstances, not courtship. Ingredients like these had delighted audiences in *The 39 Steps* and *Young and Innocent*, and they did so again in *The Lady Vanishes*, which fleshes out its picaresque plot with splendid performances by charming Lockwood, motherly Whitty, droll Radford and Wayne, and suave, dashing Redgrave in his first movie role.

The five years that produced the classic thriller sextet were crucial ones for Hitchcock, consolidating his expertise in the delicate art of giving moviegoers the tested formulas they loved while continually refreshing the patterns with unexpected twists, tones, and textures. Common elements run through the six pictures, as Charles Barr notes in his book on the director's British films: most are loosely based on novels, are primarily scripted by Bennett, take place in present-day Britain or Europe, have political overtones, and join the main characters into a couple by the end.[11] Their consistency notwithstanding, however, the films remain evergreen for viewers, and attempts to remake them have always come up short.[12] The exception is Hitchcock's sole remake, the 1956 version of *The Man Who Knew Too Much*, and even there the later version's superiority is far from clear, as we shall see.

Jamaica Inn closes the 1930s

Hitchcock would apply, modify, refine, and add to his characteristic strategies in a multitude of ways throughout his subsequent career, but not always as successfully as he might have wished. The last Hitchcock film of the 1930s, *Jamaica Inn*, looked terrific on the drawing board. It was produced by the eminent Erich Pommer; adapted from a richly dramatic 1936 novel by Daphne du Maurier; scripted by Sidney Gilliat and Joan Harrison; and photographed by Bernard Knowles and Harry Stradling. It sports a spare music score by Eric Fenby, the former amanuensis for Frederick Delius, and it stars the luminous Charles Laughton and the 18-year-old Maureen O'Hara, supported by Leslie Banks, Emlyn Williams, Robert Newton, Basil Radford, and other colorful players. Despite these assets, though, the film looked far from terrific on the screen.

Like the novel, the movie centers on Mary Yellan (O'Hara), a young woman compelled by circumstances to leave home and resettle with her browbeaten Aunt Patience (Marie Ney) and Patience's brutal husband, Joss Merlyn (Banks), in a godforsaken inn on the Cornish coast. There she discovers that Joss leads a band of evil rogues who enrich themselves by fomenting shipwrecks on the offshore rocks, killing any victims who don't drown and pocketing whatever loot they find. Mary's harrowing adventures put her in close contact with Joss's awful crew, his ne'er-do-well brother, Jem (Newton), and other denizens of the inn's inhospitable milieu. Laughton portrays Sir Humphrey Pengallan, a hugely supercilious aristocrat. Sir Humphrey replaces the novel's nasty vicar, since a nasty vicar would have run aground on the shoals of Hollywood censorship.

Blame for the film's bad outcome was laid at Laughton's feet. He and Pommer had recently set up Mayflower Pictures, a British production company, and this encouraged him (if encouragement were needed) to act as a second (uncredited) producer and meddle with Hitchcock's plans and decisions. Early on, he decided not to play Joss, as originally agreed, instead taking the role of Sir Humphrey and insisting on rewrites to make his character more important. Laughton then fussed interminably about the squire's stride, allowing Hitchcock to film nothing but his face until he found the fastidious walk he was looking for; it was "inspired by the beat of a little German waltz" that he "whistled ... as he waddled about the room," according to the fed-up director.[13]

Hitchcock had always scorned costume pictures, saying he never understood how the complicatedly clothed characters could go to the bathroom. Traversing the stormy seas of *Jamaica Inn* could hardly have altered his view; even though the movie earned hefty returns at the box office, he disliked the film intensely, and it so distressed du Maurier that she almost withheld the screen rights to her 1938 bestseller *Rebecca*, fearing that a second artistic shipwreck would result. Happily for all, the author relented, and Hitchcock turned *Rebecca* into a splendid film, capturing Hollywood's enduring affection in the process. Again, however, a pushy collaborator stood between him and his vision, and the high-powered David O. Selznick was definitely not a mogul to trifle with.

5

Hollywood

B y the time of the classic thriller sextet, Hitchcock wasn't just a movie director. He was a total filmmaker with a comprehensive understanding of the entire production, distribution, and exhibition process, from scripting and casting to marketing and advertising.[1] When the opening titles rolled, however, his name appeared only under the "directed by" marker.

Given his penchant for planning and controlling, a desire to add "produced by" would have come naturally to him, as it had to the select band of Hollywood producer-directors ("hyphenates") who regularly did both jobs.[2] According to the Producers Guild of America, producers initiate, coordinate, supervise, and control all aspects of the motion-picture production process—creative, financial, technological, and administrative—on their own authority or that allotted to them by studios or production companies.[3] The studio system gave prominent directors a fair amount of sway over their screenwriters, cinematographers, designers, and editors; but it also gave producers a fair amount of sway over their directors.

When working with a trusted director, a producer might downplay the oversight function, giving broad creative freedom to the person running the day-to-day making of the picture. Few directors were more trusted than Hitchcock as he blazed through the classic thriller sextet, and he became his own de facto producer during that period.[4] But his producer credentials were informal. The actual producers of his films were John Maxwell at BIP, Michael Balcon at Gaumont British, Edward Black at Gainsborough, and Erich Pommer at Mayflower, and while they usually granted the leeway he needed to pursue his artistic goals, his relations with studio execs were not always entirely smooth.

The commercial and critical success of the sextet raised two questions. Where in the movie world would he venture next? And would his creative freedom continue to rise as he moved into the new decade with new producers? The answer to the first question was easy: Hollywood, the grandest dream factory in the world, was welcoming him. The answer to the second was less certain. Although Hitchcock was respected by all, Hollywood was the most systematized dream factory in the world, and the system was organized along strictly economic lines, relying on principles, practices, and procedures formulated with the box office in mind. Nobody believed in it more deeply than the hands-on producers who ultimately controlled the filmmaking process. And few were more hands-on than David O. Selznick, who had the prickly pleasure of becoming Hitchcock's first Hollywood producer.

"Directors Are Dead"

Well before he set up shop in California in 1940, Hitchcock had been angling for Hollywood, and chafing at his director-only status. His active courtship started as early as 1937, when he visited New York for a gastronomic holiday, as he called it. In a pattern that would persist for the next several decades, he used his yen for food and unabashed corpulence (then 282 pounds, according to him) as a trademark, a marketing tool, and a badge of amiable English eccentricity. The director "clearly had a game plan from the moment he set foot on American soil," film scholar Jan Olsson accurately states: "to entertain journalists while eating and turn his culinary propensities into a prime selling point for his creative persona."[5] The plan paid off. Journalists dined with him, schmoozed with him, and gave him ink, assuring that his East Coast shenanigans would make a noise on the West Coast too.

Flirting with Hollywood on a second front as well, Hitchcock floated a new view of the creative pecking order in a 1937 article titled "Directors are Dead," published in *Film Weekly* under his byline. In it, he pointed to producers as the primary creators—the auteurs, in today's parlance—who placed their personal stamp on their productions. He added that the most gifted directors (i.e., directors like him) should step into both roles, or better yet, should become writer-producers, the "ultimate ideal" for the industry's future.[6]

This argument rested on two points: that the story is the "most important" element of a movie, and that film history is littered with the mistakes of directors who "chopped and changed stories about until they were completely ruined" because no producer rode herd on them. Both points are the opposite of what Hitchcock would be saying a little later in his career, when he crossed swords with Selznick and concluded that "pure cinema" is a matter of imagery and editing, not scripts and stories. But the article showed him batting his eyelids quite strenuously at Selznick, whom he named as a producer with "flair" who "works closely on the story end of his pictures and follows them right through."[7]

Despite these efforts, Hitchcock's journey to American employment took a while. Feelers came from Selznick, the top-flight producer who set up Selznick International Pictures in 1935, and from MGM, the richest of the Hollywood studios. MGM proved to be less than serious, however, and Selznick wanted to bide his time rather than pay more than the English director might ultimately be worth to American audiences. Fortunately for Hitchcock, his recently signed American agent happened to be Selznick's brother, and the producer eventually came through. That is how Europe's most acclaimed young director moved to Hollywood in 1939, after signing a seven-year contract with a Hollywood mogul who was largely unimpressed with the style, tone, and technique of his new hire.

Hitchcock took obvious pleasure in the creative and technical resources now available to him, but he quickly discovered that he would not be functioning as his own de facto producer, at least when Selznick was in the picture. His first film for the producer, the 1940 psychological drama *Rebecca*, launched the American phase of his career with a flourish. The two filmmakers frequently clashed during the production, though, and Selznick's unceasing interference in creative matters irked Hitchcock even when he proceeded to implement the producer's ideas.

They collaborated on three more films over the next seven years: *Spellbound* for Selznick International and then Selznick's recently established Vanguard Films in 1945, *Notorious* for Vanguard and RKO Radio Pictures in 1946, and *The Paradine Case* for Vanguard and RKO in 1947. Each project brought discord and tension, and while the outcome for *Notorious* was triumphant—it became a smash hit and a key film in Hitchcock's canon—it's hardly coincidental that Selznick was absent after the production's early stages, having sold the film to RKO so he could concentrate on *Duel in the Sun*, the 1946 western that went through half a dozen directors before reaching the screen with King Vidor's name in the credits. Once again Hitchcock was a de facto producer, holding "nearly the power that came with the title" and using it to make *Notorious* "the first American picture he could call his own."[8]

Rebecca

"Last night I dreamt I went to Manderley again."[9] So begins *Rebecca*, the fifth and (still) most famous novel by Daphne du Maurier, whose *Jamaica Inn* had proved imperfect Hitchcockian fodder. Written in a speedy four months, the book was published in 1938 by Gollancz in London and Doubleday in New York, and took less than a month to sell double the 20,000 copies of its initial print run. It has been continuously in print ever since, selling thousands of copies each month in the American market alone.[10]

Rebecca is a well-wrought story and remains an absorbing read. Mindful of the novel's many admirers, Hitchcock and Selznick kept the narrative reasonably intact. The writer and critic V.S. Pritchett summarized it in 1938:

> [It] tells how a young girl … meets a mysteriously curt and unhappy widower of 40 with the past on his mind. He is an aristocrat, the owner of one of the finest country houses in the south of England. The two marry and return to England, where very soon the nice, naif girl finds she is overshadowed by the perfections of Rebecca, the man's first wife. The servants and the county drop bricks continually, and are led by a macabre housekeeper who is out to protect the memory of Rebecca from the innocent upstart.

Her jealousy is, however, mistaken, The husband is brooding not about his first wife, but about a crime. A ship is wrecked, a body discovered, exposure threatened, blackmail is proposed by [a] wicked cousin ... and only a last-minute discovery frees the husband. The housekeeper, having read her *Jane Eyre*, burns the house down, and away go the young girl and her husband into exile.

Pritchett acknowledged the excitement kindled by du Maurier's bestseller, and he foresaw its movie possibilities. "What Hollywood calls the 'twists' are perfect," he opined, "adding that "the melodrama is excellent." He attributed its popularity not to literary merit, however, but to its distinction as "a perfect example of high-class literary opiate," and he predicted that its rapid rise would be followed by an equally rapid fall into obscurity.[11] While he was manifestly wrong on the last point, his disdain for the novel is a useful reminder that applause is never universal, even when it's loud. Hitchcock and Selznick knew that missteps with their adaptation could leave them with another *Jamaica Inn* on their hands, turning a profit at the ticket window but boding ill for the future of their partnership.

The director and producer didn't disagree about everything, to be sure. They both thought Ronald Colman would be the ideal Maxim de Winter, but Colman declined the part for reasons related to his screen image. Laurence Olivier was a terrific second choice except for his resistance to working with co-star Joan Fontaine, who won the plum role of the second Mrs. de Winter over Vivien Leigh, for whom boyfriend Olivier had vigorously lobbied; he did, however, finally accept the role. Fontaine herself was clearly nervous about her first major movie part, and Hitchcock tapped into her anxieties to bring out the insecurity and self-doubt felt by her character.

Selznick was the most infamously prolific memo writer in all Hollywood, and he peppered Hitchcock with admonitions and advice on many topics, including the performances of both leads. "I think you've handled Joan with great restraint," he wrote, "but I think we've got to be careful not to lose what little variety there is in the role by underplaying her in her emotional moments.... I'd like to urge that you be a little more Yiddish Art Theatre in these moments, and a little less English Repertory Theatre, which will ... not make it seem as though Joan is simply not capable of the big moments."[12] Frictions also emerged vis-à-vis the screenplay, which underwent considerable rewriting, due in part to Production Code censorship, which decreed (among other things) that killers must suffer for their crimes. Maxim's shooting of Rebecca therefore turned into Maxim's shoving of Rebecca, who died from a fatal but accidental bump on the head. On the other side of the coin, the filmmakers got past the Code by using indirection and insinuation to suggest the doomed lesbian longings of the housekeeper, Mrs. Danvers, played to perfection by Judith Anderson, a major Broadway star in her second feature-film appearance.

More broadly, Selznick was uneasy about Hitchcock's steady adherence to the working methods he had refined in his marvelous English pictures. Hitchcock pre-planned his shots and sequences carefully, shooting a minimum of alternative footage, whereas Selznick liked significant moments to be filmed from multiple angles and perspectives so the final cut could be assembled from numerous options in the editing room. At the same time, however, Selznick wanted Hitchcock to hurry things up, and additional camera setups would have further prolonged the shoot, which ultimately lasted almost a month beyond its 36-day schedule. Even in this supposedly straightforward adaptation of a popular book, Selznick complained to an associate, Hitchcock was showing himself to be "the slowest director we have had."[13] Yet after Hitchcock wrapped up principal photography, Selznick insisted on shooting some of the material over again, supervising certain retakes himself. One can only imagine how much Selznick would have dogged Hitchcock if he hadn't been giving most of his attention to Victor Fleming's epic *Gone with the Wind*, a literary adaptation with even higher stakes for his studio, not to mention his reputation.

Whether despite or because of the Selznick-Hitchcock tussles, *Rebecca* was a triumph in the end, earning 11 Academy Award nominations, including best director, and winning two of them, including best picture, a prize that no other Hitchcock film would ever earn. Selznick's next move was to loan Hitchcock out (a common Hollywood practice) to the independent producer Walter Wanger, who was preparing a picture called *Foreign Correspondent*, far closer than *Rebecca* to the rollicking spirit of the classic thriller sextet. Once again Hitch exceeded the budget, stretched out the schedule—planned for 12 weeks, the production rolled along for 30—and labored over the screenplay, to which some 14 writers contributed. And once again he made a splendid entertainment.

Foreign Correspondent

Europe was deep in the turmoil of World War II when Wanger recruited Hitchcock to direct a project he'd been developing for years, based on a memoir by journalist Vincent Sheean that had won the National Book Award for best biography in 1935.[14] Sheean's autobiographical account dealt with momentous events in recent history—the spread of communism, the rise of fascism and Nazism, the Spanish Civil War—but its anti-Nazi stance raised worries in Hollywood even in 1938, when political neutrality was the rule with studios anxious to keep every foreign market open to their wares. Faced with losing financial support for any production openly critical of Germany's dark endeavors, Wanger finally abandoned his idea of producing a more or less faithful version of Sheean's book, which, in any case, had defeated the efforts of numerous writers hired to adapt it. Instead, he handed the project to Hitchcock with permission to handle it however he liked, as long as the result involved an American correspondent tracking down developments in present-day Europe.

This cinematic carte blanche was quite a change from Selznick's meddling, and *Foreign Correspondent* is quite a change from *Rebecca*, which Hitchcock later disparaged because it lacked his characteristic humor; wit and dash abound in *Foreign Correspondent*, which critic James Naremore has called the director's first real American movie.[15] Also different was the world situation, which makes the playfulness of *Foreign Correspondent* all the more striking. By the time of its premiere in August 1940, most of Europe was under the boot of German or Soviet forces, and Nazi planes were preparing the Blitz against London, which started a few days after the film opened.

Although the movie gives its villains a made-up nationality (they're from Boravia, wherever that is) and keeps Nazi salutes and swastikas off-screen, its clearly anti-fascist slant expresses the views held by Wanger and by Hitchcock, who was being criticized by some English observers for bailing out of his endangered country, as if he could have steered his evolving career in directions dictated solely by international crisis. He felt acute anxiety over Britain's growing peril, and the evolving moods of *Foreign Correspondent*—shifting from comedy and romance to intrigue and patriotism—reflect his effort to bolster the anti-fascist cause without stumbling over Hollywood's neutrality stance. The picture's closing scenes amount to a marvelous joke on the notion of staying neutral when what's needed is bold commitment. Forbidden to communicate with his newspaper on the American ship that's rescued him from death at sea, the hero tricks the captain into confirming crucial facts near a hidden telephone receiver. A flood of revelatory articles soon follows.

The hero of *Foreign Correspondent* is the blandly named John Jones (Joel McCrea), a happy-go-lucky reporter who's content to cut out paper dolls when there isn't any news worth chasing down. His editor at the fictional *New York Globe*, a no-nonsense journalist named Powers (Harry Davenport), has some very consequential news that needs working on, and before long Johnny is on his way to Europe with the imposing nom de plume Huntley Haverstock and the daunting challenge of getting information about the imminent possibility of war. He starts by meeting with Stephen Fisher (Herbert Marshall), who leads the Universal Peace Party, and then he interviews the Dutch diplomat Van Meer (Albert Basserman), a wise and gentle man who tells him exactly nothing. Jones also makes the acquaintance of Fisher's daughter, Carol (Laraine Day), and instantly falls for her. She doesn't reciprocate, but you know she'll eventually come around. Other characters include Scott ffolliott (George Sanders), a fellow reporter; Rowley (Edmund Gwenn), a perfidious bodyguard; Stebbins (Robert Benchley), a journalist with a hankering for the booze he's no longer allowed to drink; and Krug (Eduardo Ciannelli), an evil espionage agent.

The roots of the picture in Sheean's memoir notwithstanding,

Hitchcock claimed that *Foreign Correspondent* basically sprouted from his own pictorial ideas, worked into a screenplay by Charles Bennett and Joan Harrison, both regular Hitchcock associates, plus Benchley and James Hilton, who contributed dialogue, and Ben Hecht, who wrote the patriotic declamation that crowns the final scene. The production was hefty, involving hundreds of crew members and a literal cast of thousands. Its enormous budget—more than double the cost of an average Wanger film—paid off in the movie's large scale and in a number of cinematic flourishes that rank with Hitchcock's best from this period. An assassin strikes at Van Meer on an outdoor stairway while a driving rain pours down; Johnny pursues the gunman through a sea of black umbrellas; later he ferrets out a spy nest by noticing that the blades of a Dutch windmill are turning the wrong way; a plane crashes spectacularly into the ocean, seen from inside the cockpit at the moment of impact; the survivors then struggle to get out of the aircraft and stay afloat on whatever pieces of wreckage come to hand.

The far-traveling plot of *Foreign Correspondent* recalls *The 39 Steps* and looks ahead to *North by Northwest* in all sorts of ways, from their similar espionage angles to their marvelous MacGuffins, always an insanely important national secret that the audience couldn't begin to understand even if the movie gave more than a teasing hint of what it is. More interestingly, *Foreign Correspondent* exemplifies Hitchcock's increasing ability to weave an elegant subtextual design from strategically placed visual rhymes and echoes. A car window broken by a bullet foreshadows the airplane window that shatters in the crash at sea; unwanted notes sent to a woman giving a speech anticipate undelivered phone messages later on; Van Meer's fondness for pigeons has a subtle and sinister reflection in Fisher's affection for his dog, and the similarity is emphasized when Fisher feeds the pet with gestures resembling those of someone tossing out breadcrumbs in a park. Touches like these are among the beauties that make Hitchcock's films worth visiting again and again.

Hitchcock had hoped Gary Cooper would play Johnny opposite Barbara Stanwyck or possibly Joan Fontaine as Carol, but thrillers were unfashionable among top stars at the time.[16] McCrea and Day worked out splendidly, however, aided by the gifted character actors (Marshall, Sanders, Gwenn) who made Hitchcock's first "real American film" seem paradoxically English all the same. *Foreign Correspondent* was nominated for six Oscars, including best picture, and while it didn't win any, it joined with *Rebecca* to make Hitch a contender in no fewer than 17 categories at the 13th annual Academy Awards ceremony. This would be an illustrious showing for any filmmaker, and it was especially remarkable for a youthful director whose time in Hollywood was just beginning. For his next project, though, he turned in a much flightier direction.

Screwball comedy

Only a handful of Hitchcock films (*The Farmer's Wife, Waltzes from Vienna*) seem less Hitchcockian than *Mr. & Mrs. Smith*, his wry romantic romp of 1941. Written by Norman Krasna, who specialized in movies of this ilk, it's not a thriller but a straight-out comedy, and a screwball comedy at that—an impossible subgenre to define, although its usual elements include romance, spirited conflict between lovers, couples with class differences, strong and independent women, sexiness without displays of sex, and snappy, sophisticated repartee. Screwball comedies are comedies of manners, a centuries-old form with ingredients that one literary scholar lists as "witty lovers, the woman as emancipated as the man, their dialogue free and graceful, an air of refined cynicism," an emphasis on wit over plot, a breezy disregard for blunt realism, and (often, not always) a penchant for urbane coolness rather than emotional warmth.[17] More specifically, *Mr. & Mrs. Smith* is what philosopher Stanley Cavell calls a comedy of remarriage, focused on a couple who relinquish and then reestablish their commitment on the basis of responsible, considered love rather than spontaneous impulse, social expectation, or legal or religious obligation.[18]

   The title characters, amiably played by Robert Montgomery and Carole Lombard, are David Smith and Ann Krausheimer Smith, a Manhattan couple whose household ethics stipulate that every month each spouse gets to ask a question and the other must give an entirely honest answer. One morning Ann asks David whether he would marry her again if they could go back in time, and he mischievously responds that he might prefer to keep his freedom. At his office a bit later, David encounters a bureaucrat bearing news. A change in boundaries has placed Ann's hometown into a different state, rendering some marriages—including their wedlock of three years' standing—null and void. In short, Mr. and Mrs. Smith are Mr. and Mrs. Smith no longer. David doesn't take this too seriously, as he's unaware that Ann has received the same tidings. She spends the ensuing hours waiting for a marriage re-proposal, and when her unconcerned husband fails to deliver one, she throws him out. David spends the rest of the picture trying to rectify the situation, which means doing unexpected battle with law partner Jeff Custer (Gene Raymond), who thinks his longtime crush on Ann might now blossom into something more.

Hitchcock made *Mr. & Mrs. Smith* for RKO, where the heyday of screwball comedies was waning. The director was dismissive about it in later years, passing it off as an inconsequential detour from his true thriller-oriented path. He said he directed it as a "friendly gesture" to Lombard, who wanted to work with him. "In a weak moment I accepted," he told Truffaut, "and I more or less followed Norman Krasna's screenplay," transferring it directly to the screen because he "really didn't understand the type of people who were portrayed in the film."[19]

Perusing the RKO archives, however, biographer Donald Spoto found evidence of a different nature. Hitchcock was as keen as Lombard on making a film together, and he loved the idea behind this picture even more than she did. "I want to direct a typical American comedy about typical Americans," he said when shooting commenced. He personalized Krasna's script, moreover, inserting his own distinctive touches. When a supposedly delirious David repeatedly mumbles to Ann that they will "go away the first two weeks in December ... we'll have a lot of fun ... we'll go away to that ski resort," Hitchcock is signaling to his wife that a hoped-for trip to Saint Moritz will indeed take place, and when David recalls his original marriage proposal to a seasick Ann, the director is recalling the circumstances under which he popped the question to Alma Reville 15 years earlier. Hitchcock roguishly inserted the sound of a flushing toilet into one scene, knowing the studio would scuttle it for censorship reasons—sure enough, the sound editor turned it into noise from banging pipes—and most interestingly, as Spoto notes, he added a line of dialogue that would recur with variations in many a future film: "This isn't alcohol," says Ann to Jeff as she raises a brandy glass," it's medicine. It kills the germs."[20]

Reviews were mixed, but audiences were enthusiastic, giving Lombard's popularity the lift she was looking for after a string of dramatic films that had proven mildly successful at best. As a bonus, she directed the director's cameo, wherein he elicits a double take from David just by strolling down the street. Lombard made only one more film (Ernst Lubitsch's 1942 comedy *To Be or Not to Be*) before dying in a plane crash at age 33 while returning from a War Bonds campaign. Although it's not a major item in Hitchcock's filmography, *Mr. & Mrs. Smith* shows that his flair for comedy was not limited to amusing embroidery in movies based primarily on suspense.

Suspicions

An excellent scripting trio teamed with Hitchcock for his next foray into suspense. *Suspicion* is based on a 1932 novel by Francis Iles titled *Before the Fact*, and RKO had an adaptation in hand (the great Nathanael West was one of the writers) before Hitchcock took over the project. Hitchcock went ahead with a different screenplay more to his liking, penned by his reliable sidekick Joan Harrison, his indispensable spouse Alma Reville, and the illustrious Samson Raphaelson, whose accomplishments included *Trouble in Paradise* (1932) and *The Shop Around the Corner* (1940), two of Ernst Lubitsch's most engaging comedies. The prolific veterans Harry Stradling and Van Nest Polglase signed on as cinematographer and art director, respectively, and Franz Waxman composed the score.

On the other side of the camera stood perhaps the most impressive cast Hitchcock had yet assembled, led by Cary Grant in the first of four memorable appearances in the director's films. He was joined by a number of Hitchcock veterans including co-star Joan Fontaine, fresh from *Rebecca* and future star of an *Alfred Hitchcock Hour* episode; Leo G. Carroll, a *Rebecca* returnee who would do six Hitchcock pictures in all; Dame May Whitty, the vanishing lady of *The Lady Vanishes*; Isabel Jeans, from the silent pictures *Downhill* and *Easy Virtue*; Nigel Bruce, from *Rebecca* and also the first installments of Twentieth Century Fox's popular Sherlock Holmes franchise; and Sir Cedric Hardwicke, a newcomer to Hitchcock who would later appear in *Rope* and two *Alfred Hitchcock Presents* episodes. Hitchcock's fourth Hollywood film showcased a good deal of talent and earned Academy Award nominations for best picture, best dramatic score, and best actress. The latter turned into a win for Fontaine, the only person to garner that Oscar for a Hitchcock movie. The respected New York Film Critics Circle also named her best actress.

The object of suspicion in *Suspicion* is debonair Johnny Aysgarth (Grant), who meets, courts, and marries lovely Lina McLaidlaw (Fontaine) so speedily that she doesn't get to know him all that well. Johnny carries himself with a breezy, easy-going charm that never quits—he's a veritable Cary Grant, you might say—and Lina, therefore, assumes that he comes from a high-toned background like her own. He turns out to be chronically broke, however, as well as a brazen liar, a habitual gambler, and a sometime embezzler to boot. Lina's biggest problem is that try as she may, she can't stop loving her veritable Cary Grant, even when his old friend Beaky (Bruce) visits them and spills gossip galore about Johnny's exceedingly checkered past. A turning point arrives when Johnny dreams up a costly real-estate venture and talks wealthy, childish Beaky into financing it. Lina fears this is just a con game aimed at draining Beaky's well-stocked bank account, and her fears grow worse when various small hints—an angry outburst by Johnny, a lie concerning his whereabouts, information about an insurance policy, a conversation about poison, and above all Beaky's sudden death—suggest that her shifty spouse has murdered his old friend and is about to kill her too.

Its top-grade writers notwithstanding, *Suspicion* never quite comes together the way Hitchcock intended. Johnny's dishonesty and disrespect toward Lina are so severe that her unquenchable love and forgiveness are increasingly hard to believe and eventually seem downright foolish. Some of the story's red herrings and sleights of hand—the gleam of crazy glee in Johnny's eyes when he inquires into undetectable poisons, for instance—are as clunky as they are misleading. Beaky's naivety and immaturity are so extreme that you wonder how he, or at least his fortune, has managed to survive in our uncertain world.

And then there's the ending, which gave Hitchcock considerable trouble. In the finished film, Johnny seems increasingly malevolent, especially when he brings Lina a glass of milk that she refuses to drink, wrongly fearing it's laced with poison. In one of his best-known effects of this period, Hitchcock heightened the sense of menace by lighting the glass from within as Johnny carries it up a shadowed stairway. Lina doesn't drink the ominous beverage, and Johnny later demonstrates his pure intentions by saving her life during a hair-raising ride on a mountain road.

This is not the outcome Hitchcock wanted. As he imagined it, Johnny would be every bit as bad as Lina suspects, the milk would actually be poisoned, and Lina would deliberately drink it, seeing death as the only way to escape from her hopelessly ill-starred love. Justice would then be done in a final twist that Hitchcock described to Truffaut:

> [Lina] has just finished a letter to her mother: "Dear Mother, I'm desperately in love with him, but I don't want to live because he's a killer. Though I'd rather die, I think society should be protected from him." Then, [Johnny] comes in with the fatal glass and she says, "Will you mail this letter to Mother for me, dear?" She drinks the milk and dies. Fade out and fade in on one short shot: [Johnny], whistling cheerfully, walks over to the mailbox and pops the letter in.[21]

Three different endings were filmed, and comments from preview audiences were consulted and dissected. According to film scholar Bill Krohn, the director "really wanted Lina to drink the milk" and die for love, as she did in Iles's novel. At the very least, she should drink the milk. In an interview after the film's release, Hitchcock told the *New York Herald Tribune* that it would be logical for Lina to test Johnny's integrity by consuming the dubious beverage. "If he wished to kill his devoted wife," he explained,

> then she might well want to die. If he didn't, fine and good; her suspicions would clear away and we'd have our happy ending. We shot that finish. She drained the glass and waited for death. Nothing happened, except for an unavoidable and dull exposition of her spouse's innocence. Trial audiences booed it, and I don't blame them. They pronounced the girl stupid to willfully drink her possible destruction. With that dictum I personally do not agree. But I did agree that the necessary half-reel of explanation following the wife's survival was really deadly."[22]

The half-reel went to the cutting-room floor, and the film acquired its definitive ending: Johnny protects Lina from a deadly fall and wraps his arm around her as they head toward a contented future. It feels tacked on, and it is. But the thriller is elegant as well as flawed, and its modest pleasures outweigh its shortcomings.

Saboteur

Hitchcock's fourth American picture (not to be confused with *Sabotage*, his British film of 1936) starts with a blistering conflagration and ends with one of the most haunting sequences in any of the director's films. Produced immediately after the United States entered World War II—Hitchcock was storyboarding it when Pearl Harbor was attacked, and quickly modified the screenplay to suit the new circumstances—it plunges into wartime intrigue without delay, commencing with a fire in a Los Angeles aircraft factory that turns out equipment for military use. Barry Kane (Robert Cummings) is accused of touching off the conflagration, which inflicts a horrifying death on many victims, including his best friend. Abruptly becoming a classic example of the Hitchcockian wrong man, Kane takes it on the lam, dodging the police while searching for the actual saboteur, Frank Fry (Norman Lloyd), who betrayed Kane by handing him a fire extinguisher full of gasoline. Kane's cross-country trajectory from Southern California to New

York is *Saboteur*'s main signature, making this picture the most clear-cut bridge between 1935's *The 39 Steps* and 1959's *North by Northwest*. That said, the latter films don't have the political punch arising from the anti-fascist agenda of *Saboteur*, fueled by Hitchcock's powerful sympathy for the Allied war effort and his equally strong conviction that while an untrained, overweight movie director couldn't fight in the war, he should contribute to the cause in other ways, as British colleagues like Michael Powell, David Lean, Carol Reed, and Noel Coward were doing. The screenplay was penned by Joan Harrison and first-timer Peter Viertel, with an assist from the celebrated Dorothy Parker, who juiced up Kane's patriotic speeches and some other material.

Hitchcock wanted Gary Cooper and Barbara Stanwyck for the leads, or maybe Joel McCrea or Henry Fonda and Margaret Sullavan, but he ended up with Robert Cummings and Priscilla Lane, who suited the low production budget more than they suited their roles. Although the director got along well with Cummings, who returned in *Dial M for Murder* a dozen years later, the fundamentally lightweight actor didn't have the gravitas for Kane, the ill-treated hero of a story where the stakes are high. In a case of casting influenced by wartime sensibilities, Hitchcock's first choices to play the wealthy arch-villain Charles Tobin were the quintessentially American character actors Harry Carey or Guy Kibbee, both of whom found the role too distasteful for comfort; while Otto Kruger was always effective in those sort of parts, he was more central-casting predictable than either of the others would have been.[23]

This said, however, Kruger splendidly delivered Tobin's most menacing words to Kane, which would need only slight tweaking to have been spoken by Jordan to Hannay in *The 39 Steps* or be uttered by Vandamm to Thornhill in *North by Northwest*: "Very pretty speech—youthful, passionate, idealistic. Need I remind you that you are the fugitive from justice, not I? I'm a prominent citizen, widely respected. You are an obscure workman wanted for committing an extremely unpopular crime. Now which of us do you think the police will believe?" Here are three archetypal Hitchcock themes—the wrong man, the transfer of guilt, the fear of police—in the proverbial nutshell.

An auspicious fringe benefit of *Saboteur* was the feature-film debut of Norman Lloyd, a prolific actor who went on to many other Hitchcock projects—acting in *Spellbound* and numerous episodes of *Alfred Hitchcock Presents*, directing episodes of that series and *The Alfred Hitchcock Hour*, and serving as producer, associate producer, or executive producer of both shows. Lloyd's finest moment in *Saboteur* is indisputably the finale, when the evil, pathetic Fry hangs by (literally) a thread from a dizzying height atop the Statue of Liberty's torch, ultimately plummeting to his death despite Kane's foredoomed effort to save him. Unfolding in silence, the scene is a stunningly Hitchcockian blend of irony, fatalism, and perfectly timed suspense. Other standout scenes include a gunfight in Radio City Music Hall and a stopover with a troupe of circus sideshow freaks.

Bosley Crowther's balanced *New York Times* review called *Saboteur* an "auspicious production ... in the nature of an official report, clearly and keenly appreciative of what is expected from it.... So fast, indeed, is the action and so abundant the breathless events that one might forget ... there is no logic in this wild-goose chase." *Time* praised it for warning Americans, "as Hollywood has so far failed to do, that fifth columnists can be outwardly clean and patriotic citizens, just like themselves." The trade paper *Variety* deemed the film "a great tribute to a brilliant director" that would be even better "if he didn't let the spectator see the wheels go round, didn't let him spot the tricks." Writing in the London *Sunday Times*, Dilys Powell said of her friend's new film, "This is Hitchcock at his most Hitchcock, which doesn't necessarily mean at his best." And the prominent Pauline Kael told *New Yorker* readers that although nothing holds together in the "mixed-up" and "overloaded" thriller, there's enough scary stuff to make it entertaining.[24] In all, mixed notices for *Saboteur*, a likable picture if a minor one.

Shadows and doubts

Hitchcock took considerable pride in the 1943 thriller *Shadow of a Doubt*, which compiles many of his deepest interests into a tightly wound story: the transfer of guilt, the double or doppelgänger, the ineffectiveness of the police, the difficulty of distinguishing good people from evil ones, and the iniquity festering within everyday towns and families. Written by the acclaimed playwright Thornton Wilder—whose 1938 drama *Our Town* had greatly impressed the director—along with Reville and Sally Benson, the film is Hitchcockian to its core.

The opening scenes introduce the central characters and themes through dialogue, action, and visual style. A few preliminary shots lead to an oddly angled view of an apartment house, followed by an equally angled view of one window, and then a view of the man we will come to know as Uncle Charlie Oakley (Joseph Cotten) stretched on his bed inside. The room is shabby, but next to the bed is a heap of cash falling off a small table onto the floor. A middle-aged landlady appears in the doorway with news that some friends have come to see him. She pulls down a window shade, and when the shadow covers Uncle Charlie he rises stiffly from his bed, looking almost like a vampire rising from its coffin; these are the first of many signs—his eastern origin, super-strong hands, refusal to be photographed, and weird mental rapport with the niece he soon victimizes—that he is a monster in human form. His near-supernatural craftiness is confirmed when he easily and mysteriously eludes his peculiar "friends," who don't actually know what he looks like.

To evade those friends more permanently, Uncle Charlie sends a telegram telling his family in Santa Rosa, California, that he's traveling west to visit them. The next portion of the film begins with the same visual flourish as the first: an oddly canted shot of a window followed by a shot of a second key character, the woman we'll know as young Charlie Newton, lying supine in bed. The cinematic rhyme and the matching first name signal a strange, perhaps abnormal bond between Uncle Charlie and his California niece, and this bond becomes a tightening cord tying the characters together in a connection that grows ever more sinister, perverse, and dangerous.

Charming and engaging though he appears, Uncle Charlie is, in fact, the Merry Widow Murderer, a serial killer of rich women motivated less by greed (recall the money scattered heedlessly in his room) than by the degenerate grievances of an unmoored psychopath who regards

his victims as "fat, wheezing animals" with no particular right to live.
When his niece discovers this dread secret, however, she fails to turn
him in. Her stated reason is fear that the shock of learning this would
destroy Emma (Patricia Collinge), her own unworldly mother and
the madman's loving, ignorant sister. But a deeper reason must be
the strength of the uncanny tie between the two Charlies, sealed and
solemnized when uncle gave niece a ring that united them in pseudo-
wedlock but later—in a top-grade Hitchcock irony—provided young
Charlie with the decisive clue to Uncle Charlie's hideous secret. That
secret is now her secret, too. And if the murderer slays another merry
widow, the guilt will rest on her as well.

Shadow of a Doubt explores the intertwining of good and evil
through the relationship between the Charlies and also through its
portrait of the larger frameworks—the family and the town—in which
that relationship takes shape. For all its wholesomeness, the family
is so stiflingly dull that young Charlie's thirst for a break from the
routine virtually wills her uncle's arrival on the scene, as if she were
a prospective victim unwittingly inviting a vampire into her home.
More amusingly, her father Joseph (Henry Travers) and their neighbor
Herbie (Hume Cronyn) liven up their leisure hours by concocting
make-believe murder scenarios, oblivious to the actual fiend right
under their noses.

Uncle Charlie lays his true nature bare in a nighttime conversation
with young Charlie at a café where the run-down side of Santa Rosa is
represented by the ambiance and by the waitress, a working-class flip
side of young Charlie who melts with envy over the ring her bourgeois
counterpart is wearing. The psychopath's words are worth quoting at
length:

> You think you're the clever little girl who knows
> something.... What do you know, really? You're just an
> ordinary little girl living in an ordinary little town.... You
> go through your ordinary little day and at night you sleep
> your untroubled, ordinary little sleep filled with peaceful,
> stupid dreams.... You're a sleepwalker, blind. How do you
> know what the world is like? Do you know the world is a
> foul sty? Do you know, if you ripped the fronts off houses,

you'd find swine? The world's a hell. What does it matter what happens in it?

This ranks with the most bone-chilling passages in all of Hitchcock's work, unsurpassed for baneful horror by any speech in any movie of its day.

Young Charlie brings about her uncle's downfall, no thanks to Jack Graham (Macdonald Carey), her police-detective boyfriend. Yet while the evil uncle dies in the end, he has the posthumous last laugh when the folks of Santa Rosa memorialize him as an inspiring, upstanding figure who brightened their ordinary little lives for all too short a time. Hitchcock had ripped the fronts off these good citizens' houses, metaphorically speaking, and what he found was a dismaying mix of naïveté, complacency, and cluelessness.

Lifeboat

After collaborating with Wilder on *Shadow of a Doubt*, Hitchcock recruited John Steinbeck, winner of the Pulitzer Prize for his 1939 novel *The Grapes of Wrath*, to work up a screen story from an idea the director had been developing. The partnership with Steinbeck was not felicitous—the author tried (unsuccessfully) to remove his name from the finished film, for which Jo Swerling received screenplay credit—but while *Lifeboat* certainly has its flaws, it's on balance a suspenseful and thought-provoking wartime drama. With its action staged entirely in a single closed environment, the film is also important as the first of Hitchcock's ventures into the cinema of claustrophobia, a subgenre he explored further in *Rope*, *Dial M for Murder*, and *Rear Window*.

The premise is easily described. When an Allied freighter is attacked and sunk by a German submarine, assorted survivors hunker down in a lifeboat, hoping for rescue but uncertain if or when it will arrive. They constitute a microcosm of backgrounds and character types, ranging from journalist Connie Porter (Tallulah Bankhead), industrialist C.J. Rittenhouse (Henry Hull), and military nurse Alice MacKenzie (Mary Anderson) to shell-shocked Mrs. Higby (Heather Angel), radio operator Sparks Garrett (Hume Cronyn), working-class seaman Gus Smith (William Bendix), communist-leaning sailor John Kovac (John

Hodiak), and African-American steward Joe Spencer (Canada Lee). Later they are joined by Willi (Walter Slezak), who turns out to be the captain of the submarine that sunk their ship. Tensions were high before Willi's arrival, and after it they become volcanic. Water and food dwindle, physical ailments intensify, tempers flare, and disagreements proliferate, especially on such life-and-death issues as what destination to aim for and whether Willi's presence should be endured or terminated.

Hitchcock handled the film's stylistic challenges with tremendous skill, conjuring so many diversified effects with such measured resources—a circumscribed setting (a 40-foot boat) and small cast (nine people)—that the action feels densely dramatic rather than oppressively cramped. Although it's often described as having no music, the opening titles and torpedo scene are accompanied by dissonant tones from the veteran Hollywood composer Hugo W. Friedhofer, and music recurs when Joe plays his recorder and when Willi sings his lulling German songs. Music scholar Jack Sullivan likens the singing Willi to the singing Nazis in *Saboteur* and *Notorious*, since these "musically sophisticated villains" all contest the Shakespearean notion that "the man with no music is one who is untrustworthy." The film needs no other music for, as Sullivan eloquently observes, the ocean itself "rises in crescendo during squalls and fades during periods of calm, providing ... its own sonic drama and atmosphere." And when a rescue ship finally appears in the distance, Friedhofer heralds the moment with a grand valedictory cadence.[25]

The most complex and probing aspect of *Lifeboat* is its prismatic view of human nature. The denizens of the lifeboat hail from countries that call themselves egalitarian democracies, but class divisions and ethnic or racial tensions are always smoldering away, consciously or unconsciously, and the more their circumstances deteriorate, the more the passengers' interactions threaten to explode into real violence. The blowup comes when Willi is definitively revealed as a self-serving liar and betrayer of the group, whereupon concern for the collective good abruptly gives way to vengeance by a furious, atavistic mob. The only passenger who doesn't join in the mayhem is Joe, who has no sympathy for Nazis but knows the failings of so-called democracies better than all the white passengers put together. The patriotic paeans in *Saboteur* may seem forced and overcooked at times, but Hitchcock did a major course correction here, suggesting that ideals of essential human fairness and justice can disintegrate in an instant when pressures grow too strong. The climax of *Lifeboat* exemplifies the darkest side of Hitchcockian irony.

Reviews extended across a wide philosophical spectrum. *Variety* called *Lifeboat* a "powerful" adaptation of Steinbeck's narrative, a "devastating indictment of the nature of Nazi bestiality." But the staunchly anti-Nazi columnist Dorothy Thompson gave it "ten days to get out of town," and Bosley Crowther of the *New York Times* expressed "a sneaking suspicion that the Nazis, with some cutting here and there, could turn [the film] into a whiplash against the 'decadent democracies.' And it is questionable whether such a picture, with such a theme, is judicious at this time."[26] At that time the film proved unpopular with audiences, but since then its reputation has deservedly rebounded.

One more point of interest: in a movie set entirely on a lifeboat, how could Hitchcock do his trademark cameo appearance? The flotsam from the sunken freighter includes a sheet of newspaper carrying an ad for a weight-reducing product, illustrated with before-and-after photos of a portly man who shed a few pounds with its help. The man in the ad is Alfred Hitchcock.

Two small films

Along with *Lifeboat*, 1944 brought two additional films—each about half an hour long—born from Hitchcock's desire to participate in the war effort.[27] Hoping to "get right into the atmosphere of war," he flew to London and accepted a proposal from the British Ministry of Information, agreeing to make "two small films that were tributes to the work of the French Resistance" and could be used as morale boosters in parts of France where freedom fighters were gaining ground. The actors came from the Molière Players, a French troupe exiled to Britain by the Nazi occupation.

The films are indeed small, but they're recognizably Hitchcockian in their concerns. *Bon Voyage* centers on a Royal Air Force gunner who has escaped to Britain from a German prison camp. He believes his flight to freedom was enabled by a Polish prisoner, but after questioning from a Free French officer, he learns that the help actually came from a Gestapo agent. The film then revisits his escape, which looks very different in light of this information. The ambiguities of this story—between virtue and villainy, reality and illusion—are thoroughly Hitchcockian.

Aventure Malgache brings in another favorite Hitchcock theme—the importance of role-playing and performance in life as well as art—through the story of a hidden escape route, a lawyer who helps Resistance fighters negotiate it, and a police chief who opposes him. Based on real events, the film's relatively complex narrative and depiction of conflict within the Free French community generated enough uneasiness to keep it off the screen for the next 50 years.

These modest propaganda pictures came to general notice in the 1990s when the British Film Institute and others prodded the British government to end the restrictions on them now that the passage of half a century had mooted concerns about their possible effects on French and British sensibilities. Writing about their theatrical and home-video release in 1993, I said that although they are "minor works, of interest more for their history than their aesthetics," they demonstrate once again that Hitchcock could find ways of engaging with his characteristic themes under just about any circumstances.[28]

Spellbound by psychoanalysis

Psychoanalysis was fashionable in the 1940s. Controversial and even scandalous when they emerged in the first decades of the 20th century, the theories and teachings of Sigmund Freud had acquired a large following in the United States and Europe by the time World War II broke out. When the fighting was over, psychiatry was on the rise as never before, thanks to the successes it claimed in restoring the mental health of soldiers traumatized by the stresses of combat. Movies had been mining this clinical terrain ever since *Dr. Dippy's Sanitarium* in 1906, and the postwar years put psychologists and psychiatrists into pictures of every stripe, from musicals (Mitchell Leisen's *Lady in the Dark*, 1946) and horror films (Mark Robson's *Bedlam*, 1946) to comedies (Irving Reis's *The Bachelor and the Bobby-Soxer*, 1947) and film noir (Otto Preminger's *Whirlpool*, 1949).

Hitchcock wasn't much interested in psychoanalysis as a science, a practice, or a cure. He didn't even like Method acting, whereby actors summon up their own memories and emotions when preparing and performing their roles. Summing up Hitchcock's attitude, film scholar Leonard Leff notes that when an actor asked, "What's my motivation?" the director would reply, "Your salary."[29]

That said, Hitchcock was exquisitely aware of how complex and conflicted human personalities invariably are, and as his career evolved, he showed increased sensitivity to the psychological depths underlying the suspense and action of his stories. So when producer Selznick green-lighted a production about psychoanalytic sleuthing in a mental institution—not coincidentally, Selznick was fresh out of analysis, with good results—director Hitchcock was ready and willing to take it on. Based on Frances Beeding's 1927 novel *The House of Dr. Edwardes*, the movie was written by Ben Hecht, another admirer of psychoanalysis, and ultimately called *Spellbound*, a snappier title by far.

The picture's main setting is Green Manors, a mental institution whose chief, Dr. Murchison (Leo G. Carroll), is being forced into retirement after a nervous breakdown. Everyone is eager to meet Dr. Anthony Edwardes, the respected psychiatrist chosen to replace him. Edwardes arrives in the person of Gregory Peck, charming the staff and becoming particularly close with Dr. Constance Peterson (Ingrid Bergman), the hospital's one female psychiatrist. They fall in love, but Edwardes starts displaying strange behaviors, becoming agitated and confused whenever he sees parallel lines against a white background. Eventually, he and Peterson discover that he isn't Edwardes at all—rather, he is John Ballantyne, an amnesiac who now realizes he must have murdered the real Edwardes and taken over the dead doctor's identity. Refusing to believe that her loved one is a killer, Peterson helps him recover his memory and solve the mystery of Edwardes's death. She gets the final clues by interpreting one of Ballantyne's dreams.

The latter plot twist would have pleased Freud, who called dream interpretation the royal road to the unconscious. Fittingly, the most memorable scene in *Spellbound* is the dream sequence designed by Salvador Dalí, the great surrealist painter. Hitchcock didn't like the wavering, Vaseline-smeared appearance of typical Hollywood dreams; instead, he wanted a crisp, hard-edged look conveying the uncanny power of an actual dream or nightmare. Dalí brilliantly delivered the goods, but Selznick diluted the effect, shortening the sequence and allowing Ballantyne's voiceover description to cancel out the enigmatic nature of the images. While it's a striking scene, it's not the stunner it might have been.

Other notable touches include the depiction of a child's fatal accident and (a detail easy to miss) the fleeting burst of red accompanying a gunshot at the end of the movie, which is otherwise shot in black-and-white. There's also a symbolic moment when Peterson and Ballantyne have a romantic clinch, and the screen shows a semi-abstract series of doors opening one after another into the distance—a somewhat heavy-handed symbol of love-as-understanding-a-man's-mind, but a pretty amusing symbol of love-as-entering-a-woman's body. Reviews of *Spellbound* were generally good and six Academy Award nominations came its way. Hitchcock didn't take much pride in it, however, calling it "just another manhunt story wrapped up in pseudo-psychoanalysis."[30] It's really a much stronger achievement than that remark suggests.

Notorious

Ingrid Bergman returned a year later in *Notorious*, giving one of her finest performances in one of the greatest Hitchcock pictures. She plays Alicia Huberman, the daughter of a man convicted of treason against the United States. The character's unfortunate parentage is echoed by her infelicitous behavior, full of drinking and carousing, but her life takes a turn when she's approached by T.R. "Dev" Devlin (Cary Grant), an American spymaster who believes she is basically patriotic and wants her to work for him. She accepts the offer and moves to Brazil, where he's based. There she learns that her job entails seducing and marrying Alex Sebastian (Claude Rains), a suspected Nazi operative involved with postwar nuclear skulduggery. The seduction and marriage accomplished, she joins Alex's household and starts prying covertly into the activities of her new husband and his fascist friends.

The nuclear material is a classic MacGuffin; the uranium hidden in wine bottles is important to the characters, not to us, although it's interesting that the radioactive stuff entered this screenplay months before America tested its first atomic bomb. The film's fascination comes from other sources. One is the escalating suspense as Alicia tries to sniff out Alex's secrets without tipping off either him or his mother, an intimidating dowager played by Leopoldine Konstantin, billed as Madame Konstantin in the credits, as if the actress herself were too formidable to call by her first name. The film's other driving force is the emotional tension between Alicia and Dev, which stems from the paradoxical premise of their relationship. Dev has recruited Alicia to marry a man they both regard as evil, and she has done her job well, but she and Dev have fallen in love, and the potential sweetness of their romance is soured by the loveless sex she has with Alex and the jealousy and distaste this provokes in Dev.

Notorious was Hitchcock's first American film as both director and producer, partly because Selznick was struggling with *Duel in the Sun*, his troubled 1946 dream project. Hitchcock and screenwriter Ben Hecht struggled with Production Code censorship, which reared its head when chief bluenose Joseph I. Breen rejected a script draft because Alicia was characterized as "a grossly immoral woman, whose immorality is accepted 'in stride' in the development of the story."[31] Breen also counseled the filmmakers to check the production out with the FBI, telling them that the studios had "a kind of 'gentleman's agreement' with Mr. J. Edgar Hoover, wherein we have practically obligated ourselves to submit to him, for this consideration and approval, stories which importantly involve the [agency's] activities."[32]

One way or another, the film overleapt such hurdles and emerged as a gripping thriller with complex psychological overtones and intriguing political undertones. It earned back its $2 million budget four times over and brought Academy Award nominations for Hecht's screenplay and Rains's supporting performance. It remains one of Hitchcock's most popular films of the 1940s.

The case of The Paradine Case

Selznick resumed looking over Hitchcock's shoulder when their next joint venture went into production. *The Paradine Case* had been a pet project for the producer ever since Robert Hichens's novel appeared in 1933, and Selznick made his presence felt in the casting, the shooting, the retakes, and a great deal of the writing. Whether or not his interventions were to blame, the end product was undistinguished.

Bosley Crowther evoked an earlier Hitchcock hit in his favorable *New York Times* review of the new picture in January 1948:

> Do you remember the haunting disconcertion which *Rebecca*, the phantom villainess of that film, caused all the other characters in it, even though the lady herself were dead? Well, that is the sort of dark disturbance that the beautiful Mrs. Paradine causes all the characters in this story—only she is very much alive ... and briskly kicking, but her husband, a blind peer, is dead and she is on trial for his murder ... Slyly, expensively, politely, this picture grinds out a lacquered tale of a woman's persuasive fascination over many who are affected by her trial.... It gives a faint glint of the prurience she arouses in the presiding judge, a nasty old goat whose suave sadism has wholly unhinged his wife. It gives a tormenting indication of Mrs. Paradine's hold on her husband's valet, a man upon whom strong suspicion is directed before and during the trial. But mostly it gives a smoldering picture of the passion she inspires in the young man engaged as her defending counsel and of the torture this causes the latter's wife.

Hitchcock was less enthusiastic about *The Paradine Case*, admitting that he "was never too clear as to how the murder was committed" and that he "never truly understood the geography of that house."[33] But the film's troubles ran deeper than that, as biographer Spoto makes clear:

> From the start, the project was in disarray, and it engaged no-one's interest very passionately. That it was finished at all was little short of miraculous, for it was certainly a lame-

duck enterprise, a work assigned to a departing director by his increasingly neurotic and un-self-confident producer. Selznick's worried and worrisome attitude and Hitchcock's disgust with the content and method that were forced upon him conspired to produce an uneasy atmosphere from which Hitchcock could scarcely wait to extricate himself.[34]

The picture has merits, including an effectively brooding atmosphere, a plummy performance by Charles Laughton as the presiding judge, and some well-constructed moments of courtroom drama. The latter scenes were filmed in a meticulously made studio replica of London's most fabled criminal court, the Old Bailey, and Hitchcock shot the courtroom proceedings with an innovative technique, using four simultaneously running cameras trained on each of the four principal characters. Hitchcock griped about the casting, though. He felt Gregory Peck was all wrong for an English lawyer and suave Louis Jourdan was even more miscast as the amorous groom, who should have been a "stable hand ... who really reeked of manure," played perhaps by Robert Newton with "horny hands, like the devil!"[35]

Having meddled with the production, Selznick also interfered with the film's release, shortening it at the last minute and opening it at two Los Angeles theaters across the street from each other. His publicity campaign for *The Paradine Case* was larger than for any of his previous releases, but his relationship with Hitchcock was as troubled as ever.[36] Not surprisingly, *The Paradine Case* was the director's last film for Selznick and company.

Hitchcock goes indie

Hitchcock was now a seasoned professional with numerous hits to his credit, and he saw no reason to strike further bargains with studios or producers who might—and probably would—interfere with his creative freedom. Starting his own production company would let him bypass the system and reap financial benefits as well. He proceeded to do exactly that, setting up a company called Transatlantic in partnership with Sidney Bernstein, a film exhibitor and distributor he had known since the early 1920s. An additional deal with Warner Bros. allowed Hitchcock to work on Transatlantic projects while also producing and/or directing Warner films on generous financial terms.[37]

So it was goodbye to Selznick and his ilk, hello to the artistic liberty Hitchcock craved. The remaining question was how wisely he would use it, and Transatlantic's initial venture was not entirely encouraging. The picture's title was *Rope*, its subject was dark, and its star was James Stewart, who had returned from piloting bombers over Europe with a newfound conviction that acting in typical Jimmy Stewart pictures—romances and comedies like Ernst Lubitsch's *The Shop Around the Corner* (1940) and George Cukor's *The Philadelphia Story* (1950)—was inexcusably frivolous in the complex and conflicted contemporary world. He wanted to broaden and deepen his range by playing complex, conflicted characters in serious and challenging films, and Hitchcock was happy to accommodate him.

The fine art of murder

"I've always wished for more artistic talent," says Brandon Shaw (John Dall) in *Rope*. "Well, murder can be an art too. The power to kill can be just as satisfying as the power to create." This perverse sentiment underlies the macabre play by Patrick Hamilton that Hitchcock chose as the basis for Transatlantic's debut production.[38]

The film's first shot is a shocker: Brandon and his roommate Philip (Farley Granger) are clutching the body of their friend David (Dick Hogan) after strangling him with a rope moments earlier. Placing his corpse in a trunk, they prepare for a party in honor of their secret crime. The guest list includes David's parents (!), and the murderers put the party food on the trunk holding the cadaver. Stewart plays another guest, Rupert Cadell, the schoolteacher whose mordant philosophical views led Brandon and Philip to the warped idea that a "superior" individual—an *Übermensch* or "superman," in philosopher Friedrich Nietzsche's terminology—is entitled to disregard legal and moral codes. As the party winds on, Rupert starts suspecting that David has met with foul play, so he returns when it's over, uncovers the murder, and summons the police.

Hamilton's drama was inspired by the Chicago murder committed in 1924 by Nathan Leopold and Richard Loeb, two intelligent young men who kidnapped and killed a 14-year-old boy simply to show they could. They made stupid mistakes, were quickly arrested, and escaped the death penalty thanks to defense attorney Clarence Darrow, who rhetorically asked, "Is there any blame attached because somebody took Nietzsche's philosophy seriously and fashioned his life upon it?"[39] They were sentenced to life in prison for the murder and 99 years for the kidnapping that preceded it.

Hamilton's drama appealed to Hitchcock for several reasons. One was its sinister yet sardonic tone. Another was Hitchcock's partiality for adapting plays; no fewer than 14 of his 53 features are based on stage works. A third was his longtime fascination with performance and pretending. The boundaries between actuality and appearance are forever hazy in Hitchcock's films, and Hamilton's drama is a theater piece about a theater piece—a play about the stage-managed party thrown by the villains for an audience of unwitting participants.

Hitchcock also liked the play's way of presenting the action as a continuous flow with no time elapsing between the three acts. This dovetailed with an experiment he wanted to try: filming a movie in continuous "real time" with virtually no editing. Accordingly, he filmed *Rope* in shots as much as 10 minutes long, hoping to revolutionize the production process—and save a good deal of money—by cutting the photography schedule in half. Things didn't work out so well, however. The moving-camera shots were hard to pull off with cumbersome Technicolor equipment; the actors didn't like repeating whole scenes because a prop was misplaced or somebody missed a line; and Hitchcock reshot a large part of the movie when the painted sunset outside the set's window registered on film as bright orange, looking more like a garish postcard than an atmospheric Manhattan twilight.[40] *Rope* was Hitchcock's first color film, so fixing that last problem was especially important.

Time and *Variety* gave *Rope* decent reviews, but the esteemed British critic Lindsay Anderson called it one of Hitchcock's worst.[41] The film's combination of Nietzsche, morbidity, and true crime led to bans in Italy and France, attempted bans in Seattle and Chicago, and protests in Canada and elsewhere. Looking back at it, Hitchcock felt that replacing tried-and-true editing techniques with lengthy moving-camera shots was an obvious blunder. Only as "an experiment," he said, could the film be forgiven.[42]

Under Capricorn

It was an experiment he tried again, however, in his very next film. His last picture of the 1940s was an adaptation of the 1937 novel *Under Capricorn* by Helen Simpson, who had coauthored the novel on which Hitchcock's 1930 *Murder!* was based. The story begins when Charles Adare (Michael Wilding), an impoverished Irish nephew of the Governor (Cecil Parker), emigrates to Sydney and meets Sam Flusky (Joseph Cotten), a convicted murderer who has served his sentence, risen to prosperity, and married Charles's alcoholic cousin Henrietta (Ingrid Bergman), who is covertly supplied with drink by Milly (Margaret Leighton), a jealous housekeeper. Seeking to revive Henrietta's confidence and restore her reputation, Charles discovers that she perpetrated the killing for which Sam took responsibility. Further plot twists lead to the rehabilitation of Sam and Henrietta's marriage, the revelation of Milly's misdeeds, and the return of Charles to Ireland, accompanied by memories of the beautiful cousin he inwardly came to love.

Hitchcock was happy to bring Bergman under the Transatlantic banner, although her salary helped raise the budget to $2.5 million, and she had trouble turning her Swedish accent into an Irish brogue. Worse, she and Cotten hated the long-take filming process. "And of course the audience couldn't care less," Bergman said later. "They didn't need to see a camera rolling uphill, going under tables, all around the actors in this murderously difficult fashion"[43] She was correct—few moviegoers had noticed the technique in *Rope*—but Hitchcock wouldn't budge. On top of all this, *Under Capricorn* wrapped just as Bergman's out-of-wedlock pregnancy by Italian director Roberto Rossellini became a public scandal. Theater owners scratched it from their schedules.

Only limited amounts of long-take camerawork ended up in the finished film, but that aside, *Under Capricorn* was a critical and commercial failure. It is generally overlooked even today, and in my view, it deserves better treatment. As a reflection of the late 1940s, it shows the wartime mood of fear and suspicion giving way to postwar feelings of expectation and hope. It also casts new light on two familiar genres, the historical romance and the costume picture, by presenting their traditional settings and acting styles through the lens of offbeat modernist camerawork. *Under Capricorn* is far from Hitchcock's best work, but it offers considerable pleasure nonetheless. Hitchcock's talents were still growing, and the decade to come would prove to be the greatest of his career.

6

The Fabulous 1950s

A s the 1950s began, Hitchcock had two Transatlantic productions to his credit—one a box-office disappointment, the other a *bad* box-office disappointment—and their underwhelming performances led him to plan his immediate future with care. He and Bernstein had expected their next production to be *I Confess*, about a Roman Catholic priest who fathers a child, but Warner Bros. was uneasy about the topic's obviously ticklish nature. So the partners proposed a more conventional project instead, thereby soothing the studio's jitters, giving it an in-house production ahead of schedule, and gaining additional time to wrestle their "wrong priest" tale into a workable form.

The new project was *Stage Fright*, adapted from a 1947 novel by Selwyn Jepson, a British author who had published several novels about a young female sleuth whose energy and charm bring success where ordinary crime fighters have failed.[1] In this tale, the ingénue exonerates a suspected murderer—by cleverly posing as a servant to look for clues in a famous actress's home—while coping with the mischievousness of her eccentric father.

Jane Wyman, who had just won an Academy Award for Jean Negulesco's 1948 *Johnny Belinda*, signed on to play heroine Eve Gill, and the role of famous actress Charlotte Inwood went to famous actress Marlene Dietrich, whose seven films with Josef von Sternberg had given her so much savvy about lights and cameras that Hitchcock told cinematographer Wilkie Cooper to do anything she asked. The picture also provided daughter Patricia Hitchcock with her first speaking role, although the unfortunately named Chubby Bannister is a minor character who doesn't get to speak very much. Hitchcock shot *Stage*

91

Fright in England, where he would not film another production until *Frenzy* in 1972.

The lying flashback

Although he had worked on the screenplay himself, Hitchcock subsequently said *Stage Fright* was weakened by a "lying flashback" he allowed into the film: the murder is shown as a flashback when accused killer Jonathan Cooper (Richard Todd) describes it to Eve, but we learn later that his account was a lie. Hitchcock came to regret this, saying he'd unfairly tricked the audience by violating the expectation that flashbacks can be trusted. To the contrary, I think his instincts were exactly right when he permitted the lying flashback since it subtly underscores the film's most fascinating subtext—the ambiguous, overlapping nature of truth and honesty on one hand, fiction and falsehood on the other.

Stage Fright takes up this theme in multiple ways, from the disguise worn by Eve to the implication that London itself is crisscrossed by clashing currents of historical fact and apocryphal myth. The film begins with the raising of a theater curtain, and the unreliable flashback illustrating Jonathan's lie—told in Eve's car as it spins in front of an obviously rear-projected backdrop—is the first of many masquerades, machinations, and subterfuges that permeate the story. Hitchcock's displeasure with the picture may have stemmed in part from changes forced by Hollywood's morality police; for instance, they frowned on his plan to have Charlotte take off a blood-stained dress in front of Jonathan, and they nixed the idea of Wyman, who had just played a vulnerable deaf-mute in *Johnny Belinda*, appearing in "short panties."[2] The director's bias against whodunits also explained his lack of enthusiasm for the picture, which he made for the sake of its intertwined theatrical motifs, not its murder-mystery mechanics.

Moviegoers liked *Stage Fright* anyway, turning it into Hitchcock's most successful picture in years. Truffaut dismissed it as "simply another one of those little British crime movies in the Agatha Christie tradition,"[3] and the censors certainly watered it down, but it remains a spirited romp that recharges the Agatha Christie tradition with echoes of Hitchcock's own classic thriller sextet.

Fascinating design

> If you can meet with Triumph and Disaster
> And treat those two imposters just the same...
> —Rudyard Kipling, "If – "[4]

Those words from Kipling's best-known poem are inscribed above the player's entrance to the Centre Court at Wimbledon, where one of the world's most celebrated tennis tournaments has taken place every summer since 1877. Hitchcock took a liberty with the inscription in *Strangers on a Train*, transplanting it to Forest Hills, New York, where the famous US Open was held for many years. Forest Hills is the site of the film's climactic match, which Guy Haines, a rising star on the amateur circuit, must win (or lose) in a hurry so he can rush off to prevent Bruno Anthony, a psychopathic stalker, from planting a clue that will falsely implicate him in a killing.

Kipling's inspirational verse is too simplistic and "uplifting" to reflect the dark and complicated world of *Strangers on a Train*, so inserting those lines was surely an ironic move on the director's part. Yet they do have interesting applications to the movie. The main characters are imposters of a sort: beneath his respectable surface, Guy has a strong desire to get rid of his wife, and Bruno's murderous craziness hides behind a chummy and outgoing manner. As often with Hitchcock, moreover, triumph and disaster are so closely linked that they could almost be seen as just the same.

Variety concisely summarized the movie's plot:

> Story offers a fresh situation for murder. Two strangers meet on a train. One is Farley Granger, separated from his tramp wife (Laura Elliott) and in love with Ruth Roman. The other is Robert Walker, a neurotic playboy who hates his rich father. Walker proposes that he will kill Elliott if Granger will do away with the father. Granger treats the proposal as a bad joke but Walker is serious.
>
> Latter stalks down Elliott in an amusement park and strangles her. He then starts chasing Granger to make him fulfill the other end of the bargain.[5]

Hitchcock had called his 1927 thriller *The Lodger* the first true Hitchcock film, but when he started shooting *Strangers on a Train*, he declared to the cast and crew that "none of his previous pictures counted—today was the real beginning of his film-making career."[6] This showed remarkable confidence in a production that was still getting started, and the stakes were high. *Stage Fright* had done well with audiences but underwhelmed many critics, and Warner Bros. remained nervous about *I Confess*, so Hitchcock and Bernstein still needed to hand the studio a categorical success.

Their optimism about *Strangers on a Train* seemed justified, however. They had bought the rights to Patricia Highsmith's first novel for a thrifty $7,500, and the story's themes were right up the director's dark alley: the ambiguity of good and evil, the passage of guilt from one individual to another, quasi-doppelgängers as main characters, and a cinematic structure that Hitchcock adored: "Isn't it a fascinating design? One could study it forever."[7]

The novel centers on events set in motion by Bruno's idea that if two barely acquainted men kill each other's worst enemy, they will never be caught because no one knows they ever met, much less that they pulled off a pair of seemingly motiveless crimes. Hitchcock made changes to enhance the "fascinating design" and for other reasons—turning alcoholic Charlie Bruno into psychopath Bruno Anthony, for instance, and transforming architect Guy into a sportsman with political aspirations.[8] He also toned down the novel's aura of escalating lunacy, as these examples show:

In the novel: Bruno sees the murder swap as a game; his growing obsession with Guy's part of the bargain is a side effect of his growing obsession with Guy himself. In the film: Bruno starts dogging Guy right away, relentlessly pushing him to deliver the homicide he supposedly owes.

In the novel: Guy has an alibi for the time when his wife was killed. In the film: His lack of an alibi makes him more susceptible to Bruno's intimidation.

In the novel: Guy eventually does murder Bruno's father, breaking into his home and killing him while he sleeps. In the film: Guy enters the father's bedroom to warn him of Bruno's deadly scheme, only to find Bruno awaiting him instead.

Most sweepingly, in the novel, Bruno and Guy are ever more transfixed by each other, caught up in a bizarre homoerotic attraction, while in the film Bruno's crush on Guy is drastic but unrequited. The overtone becomes an undertone, turning Highsmith's long crescendo of psychopathology into an elegantly Hitchcockian pattern-picture.

It wasn't easy to adapt Highsmith's novel to the screen. Eight writers turned down offers to do it, some because they "couldn't visualize the story" and others because they couldn't stomach the story, perverse and unpleasant as it was.[9] After literary stars like John Steinbeck, Thornton Wilder, and Dashiell Hammett declined the job, the topline crime novelist Raymond Chandler accepted it despite concerns about the story's plausibility, and then irked Hitchcock by harping on those concerns.[10] Hitchcock jettisoned most of Chandler's draft, just as he had jettisoned much of Highsmith's novel, and solicited a script from less familiar figures: Czenzi Ormonde, who had never written a film, and Barbara Keon, a former Selznick associate.[11] The production was already under way when Ormonde and Keon finished their screenplay, which also had input from Whitfield Cook, the primary writer of *Stage Fright*.

As always, casting was crucial. Granger had given a shallow and off-key performance in *Rope*, but he's remarkably persuasive as the increasingly harassed and unhappy Guy, conveying nuances of desperation and confusion that consistently ring true. Robert Walker is the picture's real star, however. Casting him as Bruno was a gamble, since his screen image tended toward boy-next-door blandness. Hitchcock apparently detected sinister possibilities in Walker when he saw a photo of the actor looking "mean" after being arrested on a drunk-driving charge.[12] Walker isn't exactly mean in *Strangers on a Train*, but he is very dangerous and very magnetic in what must be the most fully realized performance of his career. (He died at age 32, apparently from an adverse reaction to alcohol and medication, less than two months after *Strangers on a Train* premiered.)

The film's inspired beginning shows only the shoes of Guy and Bruno, alternating in steady rhythm as they hustle to their train.

Another standout scene shows Bruno's tortured reach for an incriminating item in a street-side storm drain, and another shows a tennis match where the passage of the ball between Guy and his opponent (eerily echoing the passage of menace between Guy and his *other* opponent) causes the head of every spectator to swivel except that of Bruno, who gazes fixedly at the object of his obsession.

But the film is most thrilling in its climax. By this time, the characters' cat-and-mouse game has generated head-spinning suspense, and Hitchcock crowns it by making the screen spin—or rather the image *on* the screen, an amusement-park carousel that goes crazily out of control with disastrous consequences. The scene sums up Hitchcock's conviction that suspense movies can give us great pleasure while paradoxically reminding us that a world of chaos always lurks nearby. If merry-go-rounds can kill us, where can we possibly be safe?

Confession

Strangers on a Train was a hit, and Warner Bros. was pleased. But the studio was still on edge about *I Confess*, which Hitchcock was still determined to make. The project was based on Paul Anthelme's play *Nos Deux consciences*, which Hitchcock saw in London under its English title, *Our Two Consciences*.[13] Written in generally straightforward, occasionally overripe prose, it centers on a Roman Catholic priest who refuses to reveal information he heard in the confessional—about a murder committed by a layman in clerical disguise—and is sentenced to death as a consequence. Hitchcock liked the play's implicit message against capital punishment, and the transference-of-guilt theme emerges clearly as the hero accepts punishment for a crime he could never have committed. As his ideas developed, Hitchcock withdrew the project from Warner Bros. and set it up at Transatlantic, where he would have firmer control over it. Jack Warner was surely relieved.

Once again, the adaptation did not go smoothly, but the outcome was in tune with Hitchcock's evolving interests. Like the just-completed *Strangers on a Train*, it deals with the twin themes of guilt transference and confession, and Hitchcock historian Bill Krohn speculates that since Hitchcock saw *Our Two Consciences* in the early

1930s, the play might have been a model for *The Man Who Knew Too Much* and *The 39 Steps* soon thereafter. *I Confess* was to be a tragedy, however, with the exoneration of the hero, Father Michael William Logan, coming only after his death.

Hitchcock's first choices for the lead were James Stewart, Cary Grant, or Laurence Olivier, but the part eventually went to Montgomery Clift, whose arrival in Quebec for filming was dampened by his discovery that the shooting script was tamer than the version he'd read when he accepted the role. Instead of having a secret out-of-wedlock child, Father Logan had merely enjoyed a one-night stand before becoming a priest, and instead of being executed he was to be acquitted in the nick of time. Someone who did have an out-of-wedlock child was the Swedish actress Anita Bjork, who was hired to play the priest's long-ago lover, and gossip columnists had a field day when she showed up with baby and boyfriend in tow. This revived Jack Warner's nightmares about Ingrid Bergman's *Under Capricorn* scandal. "You simply can't do this," he said to Bernstein. "Not again. Not with *another* Swedish girl."[14] Bjork exited the production, Anne Baxter entered in her place, and Warner Bros. bought the production back from Transatlantic to keep Hitchcock on a tighter rein.

Warner wasn't the only one aware that censorship problems would loom large, and they did, even though Hitchcock and Bernstein hired a Catholic theologian to advise them on various matters. Hollywood's in-house censors and the Catholic Legion of Decency complained about everything from the cleric's one-night love affair to the injustice (almost) perpetrated by the criminal-justice system. To keep the camera rolling, Hitchcock allowed compromise and equivocation to water down troublesome aspects of the story, resulting in a moderately muddled finished film. It earned back its costs and then some, but side effects of the ordeal were Bernstein's departure from Transatlantic and Transatlantic's departure from active production.

Dial M for 3D

Always on the lookout for new techniques to explore, Hitchcock was naturally intrigued by the vogue for 3D movies that reared up in the early 1950s, spurred by Hollywood's need to revive slumping attendance and counter the mushrooming popularity of television. His enthusiasm for 3D was less than wholehearted—he thought its intrusiveness disrupted the illusion of reality so essential to movie magic—but he liked the idea of trying it out.

The material he chose was *Dial "M" for Murder: A Collage for Voices*, a play by British dramatist Frederick Knott that had been turned down by seven stage producers before premiering on BBC television in 1952.[15] Its avoidance of whodunit formulas accorded with Hitchcock's taste, and by using 3D, he could build visual interest while keeping the single setting of the play, continuing the experimentation with closed-space aesthetics that had started with *Lifeboat* and would culminate with *Rear Window*.

Making a mid-budget screen version of Knott's thriller would probably give Hitchcock a hit, possibly persuade Bernstein to reconsider their split, and definitely give Warner Bros. a first for the industry: a 3D production with prestige. "I was running for cover while waiting for the muse," Hitchcock told a biographer. "A play is a safety net picture." Yet his many stage-related films show that plays were much more than that for him, and in this case, the safety net was nicely suited to 3D, since 3D cameras were cumbersome and "within the confines of a stage set it's much easier to control the added complications of shooting."[16]

The tightly constructed story involves a scheme by former tennis player Tony Wendice to murder his wealthy wife, Margot, who once had an affair with Mark Halliday, an American crime writer. Tony blackmails his old schoolmate Charles Alexander Swann, also known as Captain Lesgate, into killing Margot, but she manages to kill Lesgate instead. Tony then manipulates the evidence to obscure her justifiable self-defense and pin a murder charge on her, whereupon she is sentenced to death on the gallows. The deception is undone at the last possible minute by clever and conscientious Chief Inspector Hubbard, a refreshing exception to the clueless cops who normally populate Hitchcock's pictures.

Writing the screenplay with Hitchcock's input, Knott could have opened up the play by turning the expository dialogue of the first act into dramatic scenes outside the Wendice apartment. Instead, the action was left pretty much unchanged from its stage incarnation, apart from an additional amount of suspense-inducing delay—and a superbly cinematic detour through the innards of the English telephone system—in the all-important murder scene. "All of the action ... takes place in a living room," Hitchcock said later, "but ... I could just as well have shot the whole film in a telephone booth.... You might say that a filmmaker can use a telephone booth pretty much in the same way a novelist uses a blank piece of paper."[17]

Dial M for Murder may not be top-grade Hitchcock, and its place at the pinnacle of early 3D is less impressive when you gauge the competition, which ranged from the heights of Andre de Toth's *House of Wax* to the depths of the Three Stooges in the key year of 1953. But there is much to admire in Hitchcock's transformation of Knott's "collage for voices" into a montage of faces, gestures, and objects enlivened by striking camerawork and movements choreographed with nonstop ingenuity that peaks when Margot's hand gropes for the deadly pair of scissors that will slay her would-be slayer.

Hitchcock worried that 3D was "a fad that would fade" and that *Dial M for Murder* would go out as a "flattie."[18] Sure enough, it opened two days after a front-page *Variety* story pronounced 3D officially dead.[19] Most theaters showed it flat in 1954, but in 1980 new 3D prints were shown in properly equipped venues, revealing it as "by far the most visually compelling of studio stereoscopic movies ... rivaled only by Jack Arnold's half-underwater *Creature From the Black Lagoon*," in critic J. Hoberman's estimation.[20] *Dial M for Murder* thoroughly deserves such praise, although Hitchcock might have preferred a more dignified comparison.

Paramount and beyond

Hitchcock was well into his 50s when Transatlantic shut its doors, but neither his age nor that setback slowed him down. His fortunes were aided by Lew Wasserman, the agent who was monitoring the transition of Paramount Pictures from a traditional studio setup, with entrenched executives overseeing staff producers, to a production-unit setup, with an evolving roster of top personnel brought under the company's banner by promises of creative autonomy and shared profits. A deal with Paramount brokered by Wasserman called for Hitchcock to produce and direct five films and direct another four. Hitchcock brought along the brilliant cinematographer Robert Burks and filled out the reminder of his team—including editor George Tomasini and production designer Hal Pereira, who became longtime associates—from Paramount's talent pool.[21]

In contrast with the stop-and-go progress of his Transatlantic and Warner Bros. period, Hitchcock's four Paramount projects rolled smoothly from pre-production to final cut. He also founded Alfred J. Hitchcock Productions, an independent company that partnered with Paramount and Universal on major Hitchcock productions. Wasserman later engineered a profitable move to MGM that gave birth to *North by Northwest* in 1959. Hitchcock then made *Psycho* through Shamley Productions, his own television company, and returned to Universal for all his subsequent films. Transatlantic bit the proverbial dust, but Hitchcock ended up producing and directing every one of his features from *Rope* through *Family Plot*, and while his independence had ups and downs, no filmmaker in Hollywood had steadier artistic control.

The case of the missing movies

One more circumstance involving Paramount needs mentioning. Acting on the theory that movies take on added value when they're impossible for moviegoers to see, five of Hitchcock's most intriguing features disappeared from distribution in the early 1970s and remained unavailable for a decade. Their removal "had nothing to do with artistic merit and everything to do with business," in the words of Hitchcock scholars Walter Raubicheck and Walter Srebnick, who explain the situation thus:

> *Rope* was ... made for ... the short-lived Transatlantic Pictures, and [Hitchcock] retained his rights to the film. In 1953, [he] signed an agreement with Paramount Pictures that gave him the rights to five future films.... [He] went on to make *Rear Window*, *The Trouble with Harry*, *The Man Who Knew Too Much*, *Vertigo*, and *Psycho* for Paramount....

In 1962 he sold the rights to *Psycho* to MCA/Universal.... By 1973 the [other] films ... were removed from circulation as the director's lawyers began to negotiate new financial arrangements for their showing in theaters and on television. The process took almost ten years.[22]

By the time the final deals were struck, Hitchcock was dead, and interest in his work was higher than ever. The return of the elusive films commenced in the fall of 1983.

Window on Greenwich Village

The first of the missing Hitchcocks to return was *Rear Window*, one of the director's greatest achievements and therefore an excellent choice to inaugurate the series of revivals. It also contains iconic performances by its stars, James Stewart and Grace Kelly, and by Thelma Ritter in a key supporting role. *New York Times* critic Vincent Canby's enthusiastic 1983 review synopsized the film, with particular attention to its opening scene:

> As *Rear Window* begins—in a sequence that is a model of condensed exposition—L. B. Jefferies (Mr. Stewart), nicknamed Jeff, lies back in sweaty sleep in a wheelchair, his left leg propped up, enclosed in a plaster cast. The wheelchair is by the open window in Jeff's 10th Street studio in Greenwich Village. It is not yet 8 A.M., but the temperature is already in the 90's. Across the court, a couple sleeping on the fire escape stirs. We watch other anonymous, heat-exhausted city dwellers come to sluggish life.
>
> Jeff, we quickly learn, is a top-notch news photographer who broke his leg while covering an automobile race for a *Life*-like magazine. He has one more week in the cast and he's impatient with everybody, including his boss (who remains an off-screen presence), his nurse (Miss Ritter) and his bright, sharp-tongued, loving friend, Lisa Fremont (Miss Kelly).

Lisa wants to get married, but Jeff cannot believe that anyone who travels in the pre-jet set that Lisa does, and who apparently spends as much time as she does on clothes, could last long in the sort of grubby, dangerous places to which his assignments carry him. The suspense of the film is provided by Jeff's growing suspicion that the jewelry salesman (Raymond Burr) who lives across the way has murdered and dismembered his wife. The film's comedy is provided by Lisa's showing that, when the chips are down, she's as capable of breaking-and-entering a possible murderer's apartment, scaling a wall to do so, as she is of wearing couture gowns. Jeff's delight in Lisa matches our delight in Miss Kelly.[23]

I would argue that our delight in Mr. Hitchcock exceeds any of the other delights this amazing movie has on view. Adapted by John Michael Hayes from a story by Cornell Woolrich called "It Had to Be Murder," the screenplay is designed to the exact specifications of a director obsessed with the act of seeing.[24]

Jeff is a reluctant peeping tom—at times he's visibly hesitant about keeping his eyes on a particular bit of activity among his neighbors across the way—but he is nonetheless a peeping Tom, trained as a photographer and skilled at spying on the unwary. The moral implications of his voyeurism are softened by the harmlessness of nearly all the behaviors that catch his eye, although the sublimated sexuality of his peeping is symbolically suggested by his progression from (1) looking with naked eyes to (2) viewing through a camera to (3) peering through a telephoto lens that's conspicuously long, hard, and phallic. The cast on Jeff's broken leg also has more than one meaning, signifying both physical disability and psychological emasculation, terrifically frustrating for someone normally inclined to action and adventure.

Rear Window is the most ingenious of Hitchcock's single-setting films, brilliantly solving the challenges of telling a story through the eyes of a character who sees and hears the most dramatic events—including the aftermath of a murder and his girlfriend's hair-raising invasion of the murderer's domain—from a distance, compelling the director's camera and microphone to snoop from afar as well. No film better illustrates Hitchcock's conviction that vision provides us with our most powerful knowledge of the world, yet is equally capable of leading us astray by allowing illusion, confusion, and misperception into the mental pictures we rely on to make sense of what we take to be reality.

When reissued in 1983, *Rear Window* had lost some of its nuances due to careless storage after its initial run. Reviewing another release of the picture in 2000, following Universal's beautifully done restoration of the film's original polish and detail, I wrote that for a less gifted director the unconventional visual structure might have been a mere stunt, but in Hitchcock's hands it acquired "the tightly wound perfection of a flawless sonnet or sonata."[25] Words like "perfection" and "flawless" may overstate the case, but not by much.

It takes one to catch one

Perhaps to compensate for the indoor environment of *Rear Window*, Hitchcock turned to bright and expansive surroundings for his next outing, *To Catch a Thief*, most of which was shot on or near the Côte d'Azur in France's sun-drenched south. Everything in the picture gleams and glistens, from the jewel thief's coveted gems to the fireworks in the sky and the light in Grace Kelly's eyes.

And then there's the dialogue, penned by John Michael Hayes with a wit and warmth that never quit. Finely attuned to the mellow cadences of Kelly and Cary Grant, he brushed off worries about the Hollywood bluenoses and wrote some of the most mischievously sexy lines in any Hitchcock picture of this period. Consider the words of Frances "Francie" Stevens (Kelly) as she cozies up to John Robie (Grant) while pyrotechnics burst outside the window in orgasmic splendor. "If you really want to see fireworks," she purrs, "it's better with the lights off. I have a feeling that tonight you're going to see one of the Riviera's most fascinating sights...."

The story is simple. John is a reformed and retired jewel thief formerly nicknamed The Cat because of his ability to sneak through the night and purloin gems without a sound. Now a new string of jewel thefts is sweeping the Riviera, and the gendarmes instantly regard

John as the most obvious suspect, especially since the new Cat is a copycat replicating John's unique style. Slipping away from detectives who come to question him, he becomes an archetypal Hitchcock hero, chasing after the real villain while the police chase after him.

Posing as an American tycoon to ferret out clues, John befriends Francie and her mother, Jessie Stevens (Jessie Royce Landis), wealthy tourists who could easily be targeted by the thief. Further adventures and misadventures—a pursuit through a Nice marketplace, a chase on a mountain road, a masquerade ball with fabulous costumes—lead to a truly Hitchcockian climax, pitting John against the copycat on the rooftop of a Cannes hotel. Also present are Bertani (Charles Vanel), a restaurateur who fought with John in the Resistance; young Danielle Foussard (Brigitte Auber), a teenager whose crush on John has unexpected consequences; and Lloyds of London insurance investigator H.H. Hughson (the reliable John Williams, excellent as always), who helps John out along the way.

This was Hitchcock's third picture with Grant, Kelly, and Williams, the sixth of 12 films he made with cinematographer Robert Burks, and the first of four that he and Burks shot in VistaVision, a high-resolution widescreen process introduced by Paramount in 1954. *New York Times* reviewer Bosley Crowther found fault with the film's color, fades, and dissolves, complaining that the director "has not mastered VistaVision. It has almost mastered him."[26] People who see *To Catch a Thief* with their eyes open will find this grievance hard to fathom, and Burks won the Academy Award for his superb camerawork here.[27]

In addition to the exquisite colors, costumes, and settings, visual humor abounds—never has a movie cigarette been doused with greater zest—and always there's the wordplay that provides the "zingy air of sophistication" that critic Pauline Kael praised.[28] One more sample before leaving *To Catch a Thief*, this time from the picnic scene, where chicken is in the basket and the acquaintanceship of the main characters is rapidly gaining speed:

> Frances: Do you want a leg or a breast?
> John: You make the choice.
> Frances: Tell me, how long has it been?

John: Since what?

Frances: Since you were in America last…

Hitchcock later called *To Catch a Thief* a lightweight affair, but its lightness is exactly what makes it such sunny, breezy fun.

The trouble with *The Trouble with Harry*

The original poster for *The Trouble with Harry* promised "The Unexpected from Hitchcock!" And ever since, people have had trouble pinning this pleasurable movie down.

It shouldn't be so hard. The film is a comedy, but it's darker in tone than Hitchcock's only *pure* comedy, *Mr. & Mrs. Smith*. And while it's often as outdoorsy as *To Catch a Thief*, the mood is autumnal and earthy, not summery and bright. Most important, the story is replete with Hitchcock's characteristic blend of morbidity and amusement. *The Trouble with Harry* was one of Hitchcock's favorites among his films, and for good reason.

The movie begins with three gunshots disrupting the peaceful atmosphere of a quiet day in the Vermont countryside. Shortly afterward, little Arnie Rogers—played by Jerry Mathers, two years before the CBS/ABC sitcom *Leave It to Beaver* (1967-63) made him a major TV star—comes upon a corpse reposing in the woods. The deceased turns out to be one Harry Worp, and several people in the area turn out to have plausible reasons for resting content with his death.

Surely one of them slew the unlikeable chap, but which one? Arnie's mother, attractive widow Jennifer Rogers (attractive Shirley MacLaine in her movie debut), was briefly married to Harry and thinks she killed him with a blow from a milk bottle meant only to shoo him away. Local spinster Ivy Gravely (Mildred Natwick) also hit him on the head when he misbehaved, and she believes her hiking boot may have been the deadly weapon. Retired sailor Albert Wiles (Edmund Gwenn) thinks he must have killed Harry when he shot at a rabbit and missed. Nor can one entirely rule out the abstract painter Sam Marlowe (John Forsythe), although he's mostly interested in getting to know Jennifer a lot better.

Which one indeed? As more possibilities, theories, and self-accusations arise, people keep burying Harry's body—no one wants Calvin Wiggs (Royal Dano), the dour deputy sheriff, to find out about all this—and digging it up again. The trouble with Harry is that he won't stay underground. And is it possible that all these nice country folks are more innocent than they themselves believe?

The most engagingly eccentric character in this engagingly eccentric movie is Captain Wiles, whose title suggests that if anyone is the navigator of this whimsical excursion, it's probably him. He doesn't control the events, of course, or understand them better than the other characters. But in many ways, he's like a fleshed-out version of the briefly glimpsed figures played by Hitchcock in his dozens of cameo appearances.

Like the director, the Captain is English, chubby, and afraid of the police, as he says more than once without being asked. He's the first person to claim responsibility for killing Harry, and he's fond of soliloquizing to the camera. He's full of yarns about his voyages around the globe, but in the end, he admits that his travels were imaginary. I've described him as a fictioneer, not a buccaneer, and I've argued that while Harry's cadaver is the movie's hero, the Captain is its presiding spirit, "a mixture of affability, befuddlement, and sly chicanery that Hitchcock seems delighted to offer as a substitute for himself."[29] Neither the director nor the Captain likes to reveal the inner depths of his thoughts, his feelings, or his tales. But both make lasting impressions on those who experience their stories.

The Man Who Knew Two Much

Only once did Hitchcock return to the scene of his own crime. *The Man Who Knew Too Much* had been a hit in 1934, and in 1956 he remade the British thriller as a Hollywood spectacular complete with a vast VistaVision screen, vivid Technicolor hues, exotic Moroccan locations, and a Doris Day pop song to hum on the way out. The creative team of trusted Hitchcock associates included star James Stewart, cinematographer Robert Burks, editor George Tomasini, art directors Henry Bumstead and Hal Pereira, screenwriter John Michael Hayes, who rang many changes on the 1934 screenplay, and composer

Bernard Herrmann, continuing the fabulous Hitchcock collaboration that had started with *The Trouble with Harry.*

As before, the story begins with a family traveling abroad; this time the place is Morocco, and the tourists are physician Ben McKenna (Stewart), his vocalist wife Jo (Day), and their young son Hank (Christopher Olsen). And again, a fatally wounded stranger spills a secret to Ben about an imminent political assassination. Ben and Jo should obviously call the cops, but that option vanishes when they learn that their new British acquaintances, Edward and Lucy Drayton (Bernard Miles and Brenda de Banzie), have kidnaped Hank to keep them silent. Both versions stage the assassination during a concert in London's fabled Royal Albert Hall, where the killers expect a cymbal clash to drown out their gunshot. The remake replaces the 1934 film's overlong final shootout with a suspense scene in an embassy, followed by one of the snappiest endings in any Hitchcock film.

The remake has numerous clever touches not present in the original. Before the stranger Louis Bernard (Daniel Gelin) imparts his secret about the assassination, for instance, he befriends Ben and Jo disguised as an Arab, and his true ethnicity is revealed only when Ben's fingers smear the man's makeup as he dies. The bravura set piece in the concert hall is also amplified and expanded, building anticipation of the lethal gunshot not with a conventional ticking clock but with huge close-ups of musical notes, marking off the beats until the fateful cymbals crash. (The piece being played is *The Storm Cloud*, a cantata written for the 1934 film by Arthur Benjamin; the conductor leading the London Symphony Orchestra in the remake is Herrmann in a rare on-screen appearance.)

These moments work beautifully, and many classic Hitchcock themes are at play. His conviction that knowledge equals danger is embedded right in the title, for instance, and guilt is transferred from the would-be killers to Ben and Jo, whose decision to keep quiet means they'll share the blame if the assassins succeed. Despite all this, the 1956 version of *The Man Who Knew Too Much* falls short of Hitch's best 1950s films, just as the 1934 version ranks below his best pictures of the 1930s. The movie strives too hard to be dazzling, and while Day does well in glossy Rock Hudson comedies like Delbert Mann's

Lover Come Back (1961) and musicals like George Abbott and Stanley Donen's *The Pajama Game* (1957), in thrillers like *The Man Who Knew Too Much* and David Miller's slightly later *Midnight Lace* (1960) she lacks the necessary dramatic heft. She gives a beguiling rendition of "Que Sera, Sera (Whatever Will Be, Will Be)," but that's not enough to lift Hitchcock's lone remake into the heavens.

Hitchcock and Kafka

No film better expresses Hitchcock's lifelong anxiety about the police than his 1956 drama *The Wrong Man*, a brooding and melancholy tale that strikes a stark contrast with colorful yarns like *To Catch a Thief* and *The Trouble with Harry*. Hitchcock indicates its unique place among his films by opening it with a speech delivered directly to the camera:

> This is Alfred Hitchcock speaking. In the past, I have given you many kinds of suspense pictures. But this time, I would like you to see a different one. The difference lies in the fact that this is a true story, every word of it. And yet it contains elements that are stranger than all the fiction that has gone into many of the thrillers that I've made before.

A printed text then sets the time and place with documentary-style exactitude: "The early morning hours of January the fourteenth, nineteen hundred and fifty-three, a day in the life of Christopher Emmanuel Balestrero that he will never forget…"

As all this suggests, *The Wrong Man* is less a thriller than a procedural, following a case of wrongful arrest and mistaken identity with an obsessive care that bespeaks Hitchcock's passionate interest in the story, which he learned about from a *Life* magazine article ("A Case of Identity" by Herbert Brean, published on June 29, 1953) that Maxwell Anderson and Angus MacPhail used as the basis for their screenplay. Shooting in black and white rather than the lively color of his last few pictures, Hitchcock filmed various scenes in locations related to the actual events, including Manhattan's famous Stork Club, where the main character earns his living. Yet the film is a Hollywood melodrama at heart, moodily photographed by Robert Burks, underscored by Herrmann's atmospheric music, and acted by a first-rate cast.

Christopher Emmanuel Balestrero (Henry Fonda), known as Manny to friends and family, is a musician who plays bass at the Stork Club to support his wife Rose (Vera Miles) and their two kids. Rose has dental problems, and her aching teeth require some pricey treatment. Inquiring about a loan at an insurance office, Manny gets mistaken for a thief who has committed a string of robberies in the area. Police arrest him, question him, and decide he's a likely suspect. It doesn't help that Manny flunks a test designed to compare his handwriting with the writing on a holdup note, misspelling a word (writing "draw" instead of "drawer") the same way the real thief did.

Eventually released on bail, Manny hires lawyer Frank D. O'Connor (Anthony Quayle) to defend him, but problems plague him at every turn: tracking down alibi witnesses is drudgery; some of them have died; and when he finally gets into court, a juror's misconduct invalidates the trial, which has to start all over again. Manny slogs dutifully along, desperately hoping to clear his name, but Rose succumbs to despair, becoming so depressed that Manny commits her to a sanitarium. When his long-delayed exoneration finally comes, it seems as arbitrary as the mistakes and coincidences that crushed him in the first place: his old Italian mother advises him to pray, and as he kneels in his room, the real crook is caught red-handed in another robbery, clearing up the confusion at last.

Happy ending. Or is it? The ordeal has devastated Manny's home, driven his wife literally insane, and taken an unimaginable toll on his own mental health. Hitchcock follows Hollywood convention (and the facts of the original case) by tacking on a final shot of the family starting a new life in Florida, accompanied by a text saying Rose has been cured, but the image has a remote and chilly look, and the reassurance about Rose is unconvincing.

Hitchcock doesn't pack his films with literary references, but when he made *The Wrong Man* he must have thought of Franz Kafka, the supreme chronicler of social, cultural, and juridical absurdity in the contemporary world. Manny's tribulations are less nightmarish than the afflictions suffered by the foredoomed hero of Kafka's towering

1925 novel *The Trial*, but the echoes are undeniable. The harder Manny tries to live the upright life of a hard-working family man, the more snares, pitfalls, and obstacles spring up in his path; and the more the authorities aim to follow the rules, the more misleading and unfair the results seem to be. In the end, nobody but God can untangle the mess, and it's a good thing God happens to be listening, rare as that is in a Hitchcock movie.

The Wrong Man is one part documentary, one part Kafka, and one part cautionary tale, warning us that we could all share (Every-)Manny's fate if the American Dream should suddenly turn sour. But mainly it's pure Hitchcock, engrossing and unnerving in equal measure.

Scottie's lying eyes

After promoting *The Wrong Man* as a true tale steeped in authenticity, Hitchcock turned to a story that's low on real-world plausibility but extremely high in mesmerizing dramatic power. *Vertigo* is also a compendium of classic Hitchcock themes, centering on the powers and problems of romantic love, the temptations of fantasy and illusion, and the countless ways in which the act of seeing can enlighten, mislead, and betray us.

James Stewart, the quintessential Hitchcock actor by 1958, plays John "Scottie" Ferguson, a conscientious detective who's profoundly traumatized by seeing a fellow cop fall to his death during a rooftop chase. After retiring from the police, Scottie hears from an old college chum named Gavin Elster (Tom Helmore), who wants an investigator to look into a very unusual situation. Elster avers that his wife, Madeleine (Kim Novak), has been possessed by the spirit of a crazy, unhappy great-grandmother she never knew. Now the long-dead woman may be luring Madeleine toward suicide, and even if this is all a figment of Madeleine's imagination, tragedy might occur if no one intervenes.

Scottie is skeptical, but the moment he sees Madeleine he falls in love. He accepts the assignment, spies on Madeleine from afar, and eventually gets to know her up close. The plot reaches a tipping point when she slips from his grasp and races up the bell tower of an old church, apparently driven by her ancestor's demonic spirit. Frozen by his acrophobia, Scottie looks on in horror as another deadly fall takes place before his eyes.

After suffering a mental breakdown as a result, Scottie takes to roaming around the city much as Madeleine did. When he meets a young woman named Judy who looks almost exactly like his lost love, he loses no time persuading her to adopt Madeleine's clothing, hairstyle, and demeanor. But now a flashback reveals—to us, not to Scottie—that Judy and Madeleine are the same person. Hired by Elster as part of a scheme to kill his wife, Judy masqueraded as Madeleine so Scottie would bring her to the bell tower, knowing his fear of heights would keep him from seeing Elster throw the real Madeleine to her death. When a careless slip by Judy gives Scottie a clue to the truth, he forces her to the tower for a last climb up the fatal stairs.

The most memorable shots in *Vertigo* are the ones capturing Scottie's vertigo at moments of crisis. In the most brilliant of all his Hitchcock collaborations, cinematographer Burks created these dizzying images by combining two contradictory techniques, artificially *zooming in* with an adjustable lens while physically *tracking back* with the camera on a dolly. These shots make the screen itself seem to share Scottie's acrophobic terror, and more important, they convey the cruel psychological clash between his feelings of *attraction* and *repulsion* toward Madeleine/Judy, who becomes his seducer, his lover, his betrayer, and his tormenter as their relationship evolves.

Other key contributors include composer Herrmann, whose hypnotic score instills an eerie, disoriented mood from its first notes, and the astoundingly imaginative Saul Bass, whose opening titles set the tone for Scottie's dazed enthrallment with a slow succession of circling swirls and spirals. *Vertigo* was adapted by screenwriters Alec Coppell and Samuel Taylor from the novel *D'Entre les morts* (*From Among the Dead*) by the French crime writers Pierre Boileau and Thomas Narcejac, who wrote the tale with Hitchcock specifically in mind, knowing how much he admired Henri-Georges Clouzot's thriller *Diaboloque* (1955), also based on one of their novels. They were right: the tale was made to order for the master of suspense, and he worked the feeling of vertigo into every aspect of the film, from its

San Francisco setting (hills and more hills) to the swirl in Madeleine's hairdo.

When movie critics are polled about their all-time favorites, *Vertigo* routinely comes in at or near first place. Yet the film was a critical and commercial flop in 1958, for more than one reason. Aware that many fans were put off by *The Wrong Man*, Paramount's publicity touted *Vertigo* as a romantic thriller in the time-honored Hitchcock vein, leaving audiences unprepared for its deliberate pace and obsessive atmosphere. When ticket sales started off weakly, the studio replaced the original promotional posters—showing two silhouettes against an abstract spiral—with ads highlighting the San Francisco locations, murder-mystery plot, and glamorous stars. But such efforts were futile: *Vertigo* departed sharply from ordinary high-octane thrillers, and there was no avoiding that simple fact.

Today we know better. *Vertigo* is a luminous, engrossing journey to the inner depths of a man whose love for a dead woman becomes the passion of his life. Capturing the story's essence, screenwriter Taylor once suggested an alternate title that could never have gotten past the censors: "To Lay a Ghost."

"I am but mad north-north-west…"

Anyone thinking that Hitchcock had forgotten how to make a totally Hitchcockian comic-romantic thriller must have been mad north-north-west (in Hamlet's words) and every other direction too.[30] Swerving away from the introspective mood of his two previous pictures, he set to work on an original screenplay by Ernest Lehman, a gifted writer whose movie credits ranged from Robert Wise's drama *Executive Suite* (1954) and Billy Wilder's comedy *Sabrina* (1954) to Walter Lang's musical *The King and I* (1956) and Alexander Mackendrick's scathing satire *Sweet Smell of Success* (1957). Hitchcock refined the script with Lehman while assembling a dream cast to bring it alive. It included debonair Cary Grant, suave James Mason, charming Eva Marie Saint, menacing Martin Landau, patrician Leo G. Carroll, and persnickety Jessie Royce Landis, among others. Also on board were cinematographer Burks, editor Tomasini, and composer Herrmann, who traded the vertiginous tones of *Vertigo* for some of the most excitingly dynamic music of his illustrious career.

This looked great on paper, and it looks even greater on the screen. Grant plays Roger O. Thornhill, a New York advertising executive who gets mistaken for someone named George Kaplan, apparently a spy with murderous enemies on his trail. Trying to stay alive and figure out who Kaplan is, Roger lands on the front page of every newspaper in the land when a photographer snaps him in the United Nations building with a knife in his hand, a corpse at his feet, and no way to convince the world that he's done absolutely nothing wrong. Nor do his problems go away when it turns out there's no such person as Kaplan in the first place.

If there's any way out of these escalating dilemmas, Roger never learned it in advertising school. Like the hero of *The 39 Steps* a quarter-century earlier, he evades cops and crooks while chasing salvation along a winding itinerary full of unexpected destinations. Along the way he falls in love with Eve Kendall (Saint), a lovely stranger on a train, and spars with Phillip Vandamm (Mason), an espionage agent who happens to be Eve's boyfriend. It all works out in the end, but it's a wild ride while it lasts.

Roger is a Mad Man in two senses, a Madison Avenue exec caught by the insane confusions that justify the Shakespeare allusion in the movie's title. While he's super-sophisticated on the surface, his middle initial—an O that stands for "nothing," he explains—signifies his inner hollowness, and his initials as a group—ROT—spell it out more plainly still. On its deeper levels, *North by Northwest* traces his progression from urbane but empty businessman to quick-witted, risk-taking hero who saves the day for all concerned, even though he himself needs saving by an intelligence operative in the climactic scene.

As interesting as those levels are, what everyone remembers about *North by Northwest* is the nonstop excitement of a tale so fast-moving that most moviegoers miss pivotal details—how Roger gets mistaken for Kaplan, for instance—until a second or third viewing, but gladly let that pass as the action takes them in its grip. The film's enormous popularity again justifies Hitchcock's disdain for the Plausibles, the nit-picking spectators who let trifles distract them from the experience as a whole. No picture by Hitchcock—or by anyone—barrels along with more irresistible momentum than *North by Northwest*, which ranks with his top achievements of the 1950s.

"Good evening, ladies and gentlemen."

Before we bid a fond farewell to Hitchcock's greatest decade, attention must be paid to his television work in the 1950s, when he and his colleagues churned out 360 episodes of two shows: *Alfred Hitchcock Presents*, which aired 25-minute episodes on CBS and NBC from 1955 to 1962, and *The Alfred Hitchcock Hour*, the same program writ a little larger, airing 50-minute episodes on the same networks from 1962 to 1965. Despite their small-screen aesthetics and Eisenhower-era propriety, the shows have remained popular via syndicated reruns and video editions.

The level of success varied from week to week, as one sees in two wildly contrasting episodes from the inaugural season: in the chillingly intense debut episode, "Revenge," a husband (Ralph Meeker) hunts for the man who raped his wife (Vera Miles); in the clumsily comical third episode, "Triggers in Leash," two cowboys (Gene Barry and Darren McGavin) get stuck in a stupid showdown that never gets to the shooting stage. The show's overall quality was good to middling, in my view, with occasional bursts of excellence and infrequent eruptions of awfulness.

Again displaying his expertise in personal and corporate promotion, Hitchcock ensured his lasting media fame by starting each episode with a little speech to the audience. His genteel "Good evening..." became another well-known trademark, and viewers loved it when he poked fun at the sponsors and commercials. He also returned at the end, often pointing out the unhappy fate of the villain, who had to be definitively punished under network morality rules.

Among the few TV episodes that Hitchcock personally directed, most were for *Alfred Hitchcock Presents*, and some of these are superb. My favorites are "The Case of Mr. Pelham" (1955), a genuinely weird drama starring Tom Ewell as a businessman with a doppelgänger; "Mrs. Bixby and the Colonel's Coat" (1960), which has a terrific last-minute twist; and two episodes that are almost legendary: "Breakdown"

(1955), with Joseph Cotten as an uncaring man in desperate need of care, and "Lamb to the Slaughter" (1958), with Barbara Bel Geddes as an ordinary woman who pulls off a perfect murder. Hitchcock directed a handful of episodes for other series as well.

Although he devoted most of his energies to the big screen, Hitch's best TV episodes bespeak considerable respect for the living-room screen. His first theatrical picture of the 1960s, an explosive item titled *Psycho*, combined television techniques with feature-film size and impact, revolutionizing the very nature of the thriller.

7

From *Psycho* to *Family Plot*

The last two decades of Hitchcock's career were the best and worst of times—starting and ending with a bang, slumping in the middle. By any standard, 1960 was a pivotal year. Riding high on the critical and commercial acclaim for *North by Northwest*, he chose not to top that gloriously polished masterpiece, which would probably have been impossible anyway, even for him. Instead, he made the extraordinary *Psycho*, an entirely different kind of picture. The images of *North by Northwest* bedazzle the eye with color, while those of *Psycho* swim in somber black and white; the former film races from one sensational location to another, while the crucial scenes in the latter take place in a third-rate motel and the confines of a house long past its prime; the 1959 movie abounds with action-packed set pieces—a murder in the United Nations, a drunken drive on a mountain road, an attack by a poison-spewing plane, a climactic chase atop Mount Rushmore—while the 1960 film presents a killing in a cramped bathroom and a scream-inducing discovery in a claustrophobic fruit cellar.

Everything about *Psycho* seems strange in one way or another, including its origin in a 1959 novel by Robert Bloch, an efficient little shocker written in less-than-deathless prose. Sample:

> Mary started to scream, and then the curtains parted further and a hand appeared, holding a butcher's knife. It was the knife that, a moment later, cut off her scream.[1]

And her head.

According to studio documents, Paramount considered buying the rights to the novel before Hitchcock learned about the book, but a scout thought the story could never work on screen: "Too repulsive for films, and rather shocking even to a hardened reader."[2] Such was the material that one of Hollywood's most illustrious artists chose to adapt at one of the loftiest points in his career.

Scripted by Joseph Stefano, the film begins with Marion Crane (Janet Leigh) and Sam Loomis (John Gavin) having postcoital chitchat in a Phoenix, Arizona, hotel room. They'd like to get married, but he's too much in debt. Returning to the real-estate office where she works, Marion impulsively pockets a bundle of cash she's been asked to deposit in the bank. Driving to Sam's place in Fairvale, California, she hides the money in a rolled-up newspaper and trades in her car to avoid being spotted by the police.

The next night Marion loses her way in a rainstorm and stops at a lonely motel. A conversation with the young and personable manager, Norman Bates (Anthony Perkins), touches her conscience, and she resolves to go back to Phoenix and return the money. Before leaving she washes up in her motel-room shower, not knowing that seemingly harmless Norman is spying on her through a peephole. Suddenly a knife-wielding female figure—presumably Norman's dotty old mother—enters the bathroom and savagely stabs Marion to death. The rest of the film follows Sam and Marion's sister, Lila (Vera Miles), as they search for the missing woman with temporary help from Milton Arbogast (Martin Balsam), a detective. The story culminates with a hair-raising revelation in the basement of Norman's house.

A nasty little film

Well aware that he was embarking on a risky voyage, Hitchcock decided to make *Psycho* with rough-and-ready techniques that matched its rough-and-ready content. In the words of Stephen Rebello, the film's most thorough historian, he resolved to "plan his new production as scrupulously as he would any big-budget feature film, but shoot it quickly and inexpensively, almost like an expanded episode of his TV series."[3] Accordingly, principal photography was scheduled at the Universal-International backlot, where episodes of

Alfred Hitchcock Presents were filmed. Much of the production staff came from the show's crew—cinematographer John L. Russell had lensed more than 50 episodes, and Florence Bush had styled hair for scores of them—and Hitchcock waived his fee in exchange for a percentage of the movie, which worked out exceedingly well for him.

In addition, the cast included no top-dollar stars. Today it's impossible to think of Perkins and Leigh without remembering Norman Bates and Marion Crane, but they didn't rank with James Stewart, Grace Kelly, or Cary Grant as 1950s superstars. Ditto for Gavin, who wasn't even a very skillful actor, and for Miles, once seen by Hitchcock as a superstar in the making but lowered to his B list when pregnancy prevented her from starring in *Vertigo* as he had expected.

Psycho opened at two Manhattan theaters and then expanded to locations across the country, saturating the market before its sharp edges could be dulled by what we now call spoilers. (Before the old business model was upended in 1975 by Steven Spielberg's *Jaws*, saturation meant hundreds of theaters, not thousands.) Reviews were mixed. "A nasty little film," hissed *Esquire* critic Dwight Macdonald, "a reflection of a most unpleasant mind, a mean, sly, sadistic little mind." At the other end of the spectrum, Andrew Sarris used his first-ever review for *The Village Voice* to place *Psycho* in "the same creative rank as the great European films," declaring that it "should be seen at least three times by any discerning film-goer."[4] Bosley Crowther of *The New York Times* said that the "obviously low-budget job" was prone to "old-fashioned melodramatics" and seemed "slowly paced for Mr. Hitchcock and given over to a lot of small detail."[5] A few months later, the self-correcting Crowther named the "expert and sophisticated" picture one of the year's ten best.[6]

Moviegoers showed up in droves, enticed by the first major promotional campaign that Hitchcock personally supervised, complete with instructions telling exhibitors to keep the lights off for 30 seconds after the end titles. "During these 30 seconds of stygian blackness," the directions from the director said, "the suspense of *Psycho* is indelibly engraved in the mind of the audience, later to be discussed among gaping friends and relations. You will then bring up houselights of a greenish hue, and shine spotlights of this ominous hue across the faces of your departing patrons."

In a further show of directorial control, Hitchcock policed the audience in absentia, rather like Mrs. Bates, who polices her son from beyond the grave. "No one but no one will be admitted to the theater after *Psycho* begins," he decreed in trailers, teasers, and lobby cards. "Don't give away the ending," he wheedled in another message. "It's the only one we have."[7]

The buzz, the ads, the gimmicks, and the picture's merits combined to give Hitchcock his greatest runaway hit; earning $9.5 million in its initial runs and an additional $6 million internationally, *Psycho* became the year's most profitable picture. And this was before ancillary sales—home video, TV showings, and so on—made it one of the most effective money-spinners in film history. *Psycho* also brought Hitch the last of his five Academy Award nominations, although neither he nor the film's other nominees—Leigh for supporting actress, Russell for cinematography, and a three-person team for black-and-white art direction and set decoration—took home statuettes on Oscar night.

Psycho and the '60s

Its excellence as a thriller aside, what made *Psycho* such an era-defining film? A full account would be a book in itself, but briefly stated, the secret lies in the intuitive subtexts embedded in its soul-jolting story, which reached the public at exactly the right time. Although the 1960s were a time of social and political commotion—bringing the sexual revolution, the antiwar movement, heightened Civil Right activism, and more—value systems of the 1950s still reigned when *Psycho* arrived at the start of the decade. Hitchcock's film obviously didn't cause the sociopolitical upheavals, which picked up steam about three years later, but the way it cut through long-cherished movie conventions pointed directly to the questioning of received ideas and traditional truths that would soon transform many aspects of American society.

In sum, there was sociocultural prescience as well as aesthetic power in the film's sly camera movements, its biting all-strings music score, its shockingly graphic murder scene, its subversive plot twists—especially the death of the heroine halfway through—and even the close-up of a toilet, a Hollywood first. What matters isn't just that Hitchcock made such a movie, it's that audiences couldn't get enough of it. Their excitement says as much about the emerging 1960s as George Lucas's *Star Wars* would say about the reborn conservatism of the Ronald Reagan and George H.W. Bush epoch.

Not bad for an $800,000 thriller that a studio report once called "too repulsive for films." I discussed *Psycho* with Hitchcock in 1972, and he surprised me by calling it a comedy, saying that if he'd taken the story with real seriousness, he would have filmed it in a case-study style without all the "mysterioso" touches. I've come to agree that *Psycho* has a profoundly comic sensibility, but not because it's funny ha-ha or even funny peculiar. It's because the deepest purpose of the film is to laugh skeptically and sardonically in the face of physical decay, psychological dementia, and spiritual death. Hollywood cinema doesn't come more thrilling, resourceful, or original. Or more subversive.

And about that toilet…

I can't leave *Psycho* without touching on the most wickedly playful element of the whole playfully wicked film. Taking a cue from Sigmund Freud, who observed that money and excrement can serve as symbols for each other—think of "filthy lucre" or "obscene amounts of money"—the movie links cash, shit, and crime into a metaphorical chain that crisscrosses the entire story.

In one of the first images, the camera glides past a bathroom of the hotel where Sam and Marion are having their tryst. That's a preview of the symbolism that gets going in the real-estate office, where a customer named Cassidy sends everyone into mild shock by whipping $40,000 instead of a check out of his pocket to settle his account.

Why are Marion and the others so startled? Because in this film money = shit, and nice people don't wave it under other people's noses; they put it out of sight and out of mind, especially when there's so *much* of it. The office boss, interestingly named Low*e*ry, says it's *irregular* to make such a large payment in cash, and Cassidy replies that it's his *private* money to handle as he wants.

Lowery tells Marion to get the stuff away from there and into the bank, and she leaves after wrapping it hygienically in paper. But then she steals it, and as she drives away she imagines how indignant Cassidy will be at how well she concealed her emotions when she saw the money: "She sat there while I dumped it out!"

And so it goes throughout Marion's part of the story: to handle the cash she goes into a service-station lavatory; when she rethinks her plans she flushes torn-up paper down the toilet; and so forth. When she's killed, her blood spirals down the shower drain, and the camera likewise spirals as it gradually moves away from her corpse—paired motions that rhyme with the water that swirled around the flushing toilet. Norman arrives to clean up the mess and remove evidence of the hideous crime that "Mother" has committed, and after scouring the bathroom, he tosses Marion's body into the trunk of her car—along with the money, still wrapped in paper—and sinks the car into a local swamp.

Symbolically speaking, the swamp is another, bigger toilet in disguise. The car sinks ... and sinks a little more ... and stops sinking, with its top still plainly in view above the surface. Norman is eliminating the traces of a horrific crime, so we should be glad the incriminating evidence can still be seen. But as noted in a previous chapter, viewers sympathize with Norman's acute anxiety every time. Why? Because this is every toilet flusher's nightmare—the bad stuff that won't go down! After a few excruciating moments the car finally sinks the rest of the way, and like Norman, we sigh with relief and get on with the story—which climaxes, as noted, in the bowels of the Bates house.

If you suspect I'm seeing things in *Psycho* that Hitchcock didn't intend—consciously, at least—you could be right. But a big part of an artist's work takes place on an unconscious level, where we all harbor dark and secret fantasies; and even on a conscious level, biographers agree that Hitchcock was forever fond of scatological jokes and bathroom humor.

I'll finish with one more piece of evidence for my case: the license plate on Marion's first car is ANL-709, with letters virtually spelling out a revealing word, followed by a number with an anus-like zero at the center. Far-fetched? That's for you to decide, dear reader. For myself, I think Hitchcock was playing a deliberately roguish prank on us, on the censors, and on the "respectable" side of cinema itself.

The Birds was coming

After a paradigm-changing blockbuster like *Psycho*, what could Hitchcock do for an encore? He spent three years—his longest hiatus to date—conceptualizing, planning, and implementing the answer to that question. When the result premiered in 1963, it was clear that still more paradigms were being challenged, if not scrapped. (Perhaps including grammar; the film's catchy slogan was: "*The Birds* Is Coming"!)

The Birds is based on an eponymous tale by Daphne du Maurier—not a novel like *Jamaica Inn* and *Rebecca*, which Hitchcock had filmed earlier, but a short story that first appeared in *Good Housekeeping* magazine.[8] *Psycho* had soared without help from top-line stars, so Hitchcock felt comfortable giving the lead in the new film to "Tippi" Hedren, a model (whose first name then came in quotation marks) with virtually no screen experience apart from the TV commercial where he spotted her. The other key cast members were Rod Taylor and Suzanne Pleshette, both richer in TV credits than feature-film roles, and Jessica Tandy, a longtime actress whose recent work was mainly in TV shows and the theater.

In another risky maneuver, Hitchcock decided *The Birds* would have even less music than *Lifeboat*, instead, using electronically created sound effects. And the visual effects would be the most extraordinary of his career: innumerable birds, large and small, peaceable and predatory, outdoors and indoors, sometimes massing in the distance and other times swooping in for the kill. Few fantasy, horror, or science-fiction filmmakers had gambled so heavily on imagery as intricate, outlandish, and terrifying as the spectacle Hitch had in mind. For the final shot alone, 32 photographic exposures were needed, combining actors, a matte painting, and birds galore into one of modern film's most memorable images.

Movie vs. story

Noting that Hitchcock's film did not please du Maurier, author Patrick

McGrath compared the (short) story with the (long) movie in a 2007 article marking the 100th anniversary of du Maurier's birth:

> The difference between the story and the film is striking, though less in the depiction of the birds' inexplicably aggressive behaviour than in the characters who confront it, and where it all happens. At the centre of du Maurier's narrative is a part-time farm worker called Nat Hocken, and in the story his struggle to protect his family from the birds is set against a wild Cornish coastline where gales sweep across stark hills and fields and isolated farmhouses. The combination of bleak landscape and rustic characters lends an appropriately elemental tone to the tale, and this is missing from Hitchcock's version, with its placid northern California setting and the urbane city folk he casts as his protagonists. This may explain the author's dislike of the film.[9]

Could be. She might also have balked at the film's unconventional structure—not as transgressive as that of *Psycho* but certainly a departure from the norm for mainstream movies and especially for thrillers.

Melanie Daniels (Hedren), a sophisticated San Franciscan, has a brief encounter with handsome lawyer Mitch Brenner (Taylor) in a pet shop where he went to buy a pair of lovebirds for his younger sister Cathy (Veronica Cartwright). Playing a practical joke on her new acquaintance, Melanie covertly delivers two lovebirds to his family's home in out-of-the-way Bodega Bay, and as she steers her motorboat back to the mainland, a seagull dives down and takes a bite out of her forehead. Mitch meets her at the pier and brings her to his house, where she makes the acquaintance of Cathy and their mother, Lydia (Tandy), a possessive widow who's immediately jealous of the unexpected guest.

Bird attacks now grow more frequent and ferocious: flocking together regardless of feather, armies of avians terrorize Cathy's birthday party, peck a neighboring farmer to death, spark a gasoline explosion, and more. Shutting or barricading doors and windows doesn't stop them from swooping in through a chimney or making a hole in a roof. The events are apocalyptic in scale and also in their inexplicable nature. Why have feathered friends become feathered enemies (or feathered fiends) intent on tormenting, torturing, and killing us humans? We know as much at the end as we did at the beginning of the tale: nothing.

Shockwaves and melodrama

The radically ambiguous ending of *The Birds* is true to the enigmatic nature of du Maurier's story, but Hitchcock and screenwriter Evan Hunter replaced the story's economical, no-nonsense style with a rambling design that waits surprisingly long before introducing the menace and doesn't unleash its high-octane shockwaves until a lot of low-octane domestic melodrama has come and gone. His screenplay credit notwithstanding, Hunter disliked the film as much as du Maurier did, taking particular umbrage at a dialogue scene (between Melanie and Mitch at the birthday party) that the director wrote himself.

Hunter later published a book griping about Hitchcock. In it, he argued that after *Psycho* the director started believing the French critics who hailed him as a great artist; consequently, Hunter charged, Hitch now felt obliged to put self-conscious "artistry" into work that was better off without it.[10] Listening to critics may well be perilous for filmmakers, but Hunter's view ignored Hitchcock's lifelong fascination with the art of "pure cinema," meaning visual cinema tapping directly into the emotions. Hunter did manage to say—perhaps for diplomatic reasons—that he loved working with Hitchcock on *The Birds*, and he strongly agreed with the director's controversial decision to leave the bird war unexplained. "Otherwise the film would become science fiction," Hunter told an interviewer, "and we didn't want to do that."[11]

Hedren complained for a different and better reason, describing the physical pain and psychological duress she suffered while Hitchcock and cinematographer Robert Burks shot the birds' climactic assault on her in the attic, a minute-plus scene that took a solid week to film. She says Hitchcock inflicted extra distress on her because she spurned his sexual come-ons, which were (unsurprisingly) totally unwanted. She still signed on to star in his next picture, *Marnie*, during which the harassment grew even worse; the tensions didn't benefit her performances in either film, which many critics (including this one) find uninspired.

The Birds got mixed responses. The trade paper Variety loved Hedren, who "makes an auspicious screen bow," but opined that Hitchcock had reduced a "fascinating" premise to "little more than a shocker-for-shock's-sake."[12] Time said Hitchcock fans "may be dismayed to discover that ... the Master has traded in his uncomplicated tenets of terror for a new outlook that is vaguely nouvelle vague," referring to the French New Wave filmmakers then in vogue.[13] New Republic reviewer Stanley Kauffmann was extremely dismayed to discover that the "dialogue is stupid, the characters insufficiently developed to rank as clichés, the story incohesive." Hitchcock's directing, he added, "has never been so tired."[14]

In a different vein, Bosley Crowther primed New York Times readers for "a horror film that should raise the hackles of the most courageous and put goose-pimples on the toughest hide."[15] And the art-minded Andrew Sarris, who was single-handedly importing French auteur criticism to American shores, praised the picture as a "major work of cinematic art" in which Hitchcock implicates his viewers so successfully that "the much-criticized, apparently anticlimactic ending of the film finds the audience more bloodthirsty than the birds."[16]

The Birds did well at the box office, finishing among the 20 top earners of the year, and its reputation has remained high. It was Hitchcock's last triumph of the 1960s.

Marnie

Several veterans of The Birds returned for Marnie, a love story steeped in abnormal psychology. Still toting her quotation marks, "Tippi" Hedren played the lead. Robert Burks photographed the proceedings, and Evan Hunter worked on the screenplay (based on Winston Graham's 1961 novel) until Hitchcock replaced him with Jay Presson Allen, who was then attracting attention for her still-unproduced play The Prime of Miss Jean Brodie. Everything looked fine on the drawing board, less so when it reached the screen.

Marnie is a Hitchcockian blonde who's not just cool but downright frigid, to use a distasteful term that was still current in the supposedly enlightened 1960s. She's also a kleptomaniac, compelled to steal and pretty good at it, using her charm to get jobs that offer opportunities for theft. She gets caught by her latest victim, executive Mark Rutland (Sean Connery), and since he's in love with her, he offers her the choice of either going to jail or marrying him. Marnie opts for the latter, whereupon her antipathy to sex becomes apparent. Mark takes this as a challenge, determining to cure her through love and understanding, which proves to be a difficult task. When he takes her on a forced visit to her mother, former prostitute Bernice Edgar (Louise Latham), long-repressed memories flood Marnie's mind, casting light on everything from her fear of the color red (recalling John Ballantyne's fear of parallel lines in *Spellbound*) to her dread of sexuality.

Hunter had disliked Hitchcock's changes to the screenplay of *The Birds*, and their collaboration on *Marnie* hit snags so severe that a parting of the ways became inevitable. The most serious point of contention was the honeymoon scene, where phobic Marnie cringes from consummating the marriage, and he-manly Mark takes her by force. *Marnie* historian Tony Lee Moral reports that Hunter was concerned about this scene from his first conversation with the director:

> Hunter felt that he would have difficulty recovering a character after such a scene, for every woman in the audience would hate him…. In Hunter's mind, it wasn't heroic to rape a woman who was terrified, and it was also dramatically wrong. Hitchcock totally disagreed."[17]

At one point Hitchcock jolted Hunter by envisioning a crucial shot: "Evan, when he sticks it in her, I want that camera right on her *face!*" Years later, Hunter told Allen how uncomfortable this made him, and she responded, "You … got bothered by the scene that was his reason for making the movie."[18] Hunter was soon out of the project, and Allen was in it. The honeymoon rape scene was made to Hitchcock's specifications, and many critics have defended it. One is Murray Pomerance, who writes, "It is Marnie's experience Hitchcock wanted to reflect in that close-up, not Mark's experience inscribed upon her."[19]

True enough, but Hitchcock's obsessive interest in Hedren was reaching a pinnacle. His sexual advances were aggressive, and by all accounts her resistance and refusal badly frustrated and depressed him. For some commentators, the film's weakest elements—the overstated red flashes, the conspicuous rear-screen projections, the painted backdrop at the end of Bernice's street—show how dispirited and apathetic the director had become about the production long before it was finished. To others, however, *Marnie* is a bona fide masterpiece, lit up by Hedren's acting and graced by one of Bernard Herrmann's greatest scores.

Critics didn't like it much in 1964. Calling it "at once a fascinating study of a sexual relationship and the master's most disappointing film in years," *New York Times* reviewer Eugene Archer speculated that Hitchcock might be "taking himself too seriously—perhaps the result of listening to too many esoteric admirers," by which he clearly meant (as Hunter did) those pesky French aesthetes.[20] Even the solid Hitchcock supporter Andrew Sarris began his review of *Marnie* by deeming it "a failure by any standard except the most esoteric," finishing his critique by saying that Hitchcock had "struck out in his own park."[21] The film did poorly at American theaters, although it fared better overseas.

My own feelings about *Marnie* have grown fonder over the years, but I don't think I will ever place it on the level of *The 39 Steps* or *Notorious* or *Vertigo* or *Psycho* or even *The Birds*. In any case, *Marnie* marked the end of an era: it was the last Hitchcock film with a blonde heroine, the last with Burks's fine camerawork, and the last with Herrmann's marvelous music.[22] It was also his last film with Hedren, although her career continued, picking up steam in the 1970s and going on for decades despite her charge that Hitchcock did all he could to sabotage it. Their relationship was a sad one, and the master of suspense bears the blame.

Torn Curtain

Michael Armstrong (Paul Newman) is an American nuclear physicist, and Sarah Sherman (Julie Andrews) is his assistant and fiancée. The cold war is raging, so Sarah is shocked when Paul abandons her—and their impending marriage—to defect to East Germany, a communist country under the Soviet Union's thumb.

It turns out he's actually on a mission to ferret information from the brilliant brain of Gustav Lindt, a German scientist who has cracked a key problem in anti-missile technology. Lindt would never share the breakthrough with the capitalist West, and no ordinary spy has enough expertise to worm the secret out of him. The capitalist West has therefore recruited Michael for his first and only secret-agent gig. His task is to trick Lindt into revealing his equations—a classic MacGuffin—and scurry back to the safe side of the Iron Curtain, from which *Torn Curtain* derives its title. What he didn't plan on was Sarah's consternation when he leaves her without so much as rain check on their wedding. Instead of accepting his departure, she sneaks onto his plane and dogs his trail, complicating and perhaps compromising his efforts.

Problems also complicated the making of the film. Brian Moore's screenplay was weak, and rather than postpone the picture until the script was up to speed, Universal pushed it ahead, concerned that Andrews would have schedule problems if things fell behind. The stars' high salaries impinged on other elements of the production, and Newman's meticulous Method acting rubbed Hitchcock the wrong way. Accommodating the studio's wish for a trendy pop-oriented score, Hitchcock requested same from Herrmann, who proceeded to write lavish symphonic music in his usual vein. John Addison was called in to replace him, and the fabled Hitchcock-Herrmann partnership came to an untimely end. In sum, more than one thing was torn before *Torn Curtain* was done.

The finished product—Hitchcock's 50th feature—is neither a bad movie nor a particularly good one. Newman and Andrews turn in mildly persuasive performances, and a couple of the supporting players turn in very persuasive ones. The best is Wolfgang Kieling as Hermann Gromek, a communist security agent whose long, agonizing death is one of Hitchcock's great set pieces, fulfilling his ambition of showing graphically and explicitly how *difficult* it really is to kill a person with only rudimentary weapons at hand. Another high achiever is Lila Kedrova as Countess Kuchinska, an entertaining specimen of very shabby gentility. Hitchcock makes too much of a good thing out of her performance, though, amplifying it in close-ups that long outlive their welcome.

In a review of *Torn Curtain* for *The Harvard Crimson*, the future (and very gifted) filmmaker Tim Hunter called the first hour of the two-hour drama "one of the most visually complex and subtle films ever made" but faulted the movie as a whole for lacking effective suspense and "a well-motivated plot, or even [a] convincing cloak-and-dagger device."[23] Reviews, in general, ranged from mixed to negative. *Torn Curtain* nonetheless became Hitchcock's most commercially successful film since *Psycho*—not the highest of achievements, considering that its competitors were *The Birds* and *Marnie*—but a welcome sign that Hitch was still in the game, if not currently at the top of it.

Tarnished Topaz

Hitchcock's second spy picture in a row received one of its few favorable reviews from *New York Times* critic Vincent Canby, who accurately stated that *Topaz* is "rather too leisurely and the machinations of plot [are] rather too convoluted to be easily summed up in anything except a very loose sentence." His sentence suffices nicely, so I'll borrow most of it:

> [I]t's about espionage as a kind of game, set in Washington, Havana, and Paris at the time of the Cuban missile crisis, involving a number of dedicated people in acts of courage, sacrifice, and death, after which the survivors find themselves pretty much where they were when they started, except that they are older, tired, and a little less capable of being happy.[24]

The film's box-office failure can perhaps be traced to the average moviegoer's instinctive avoidance of pictures that end with tired, unhappy characters still stuck pretty much where they started.

Hitchcock had burned some recently built bridges to actors of the experienced (Newman) and inexperienced (Hedren) varieties, so for *Topaz*, he wanted promising new talents who might rise to stardom on his coattails. He ended up casting Frederick Stafford as French spy Andre Devereaux and Karin Dor as Juanita de Cordoba, the French spy's Cuban mistress. Stafford was a Swiss actor specializing in secret agents, Dor was a German actress with a James Bond picture in her credits, and neither proved up to the job as Hitchcock envisioned it. The supporting cast includes many fine French performers—Dany Robin, Michel Piccoli, Philippe Noiret, Michel Subor, and Claude Jade—but the Hollywood players Roscoe Lee Browne and John Vernon make the strongest impressions.

In the screenplay department, *Topaz* had problems that made *Torn Curtain* look easy. Universal hired Leon Uris to adapt his popular 1967 novel, which Hitchcock wanted to use as the basis for a Bond-type thriller with a bit more realism than the typical Bond opus had to offer. The director and the novelist proved to be on very different wavelengths, so Uris departed. His replacement, *Vertigo* co-screenwriter Samuel Taylor, arrived so late in the pre-production process that the script was incomplete when the camera started rolling—a first for Hitchcock, whose penchant for planning had long been legendary. Taylor wrote and rewrote material throughout the shoot.

A crisis developed as the end of principal photography neared. The picture was meant to climax with a scene that isn't in Uris's novel: a dramatic shootout between Devereaux and double agent Jacques Granville (Piccoli) that the latter loses when he's shot by a Russian sniper. Hitchcock took a hasty leave of absence when word arrived that his wife had been hospitalized with a stroke in Los Angeles—the scene was being filmed in Paris—and associate producer Herbert Coleman took over for him. At the first test screening a few months later, the audience hooted the ending off the screen, either because Coleman blew the assignment or because Uris fans didn't like this departure from the book.

Hitchcock went back to France and shot a different finale in which Devereaux and Granville exchange wry smiles while boarding planes to Washington and Moscow, respectively. But this raised eyebrows by allowing Granville to escape unpunished. So a third conclusion took shape, with Granville returning to his house and killing himself with a gunshot that is heard rather than seen, since at this point Hitchcock had to work with footage already filmed. Hitch personally preferred the airport ending, but other finales were used in different overseas markets. (American viewers got the unseen-gunshot ending, although the far superior airport scene has been restored in video editions of the film.)

Writing in *Film Quarterly*, critic Richard Corliss said that Stafford and Robin convey "nothing but the nervousness they feel in characters they don't understand," that the dialogue contains "too much operatic small talk," and that the film ultimately "just runs out, like a tube of toothpaste." Another thoughtful critic, Richard T. Jameson, was more sympathetic, arguing that the point and meaning of *Topaz* lie in its cinematic patterns and linkages; when people find the film "dull" or "boring," Jameson argued, it's because they haven't taken the trouble to *see* it, to tease out the beauties of its audiovisual harmonies and rhythms.[25]

Topaz never earned back its $4 million costs, and while I don't make great claims for it today, I commend it for the riches of Jack Hildyard's nuanced cinematography, the ingenuity of Henry Bumstead's production design, and the meandering, rhizomatic structure of Taylor's screenplay. The picture has flaws, but a tube of toothpaste it is not.

Rebounding with a Frenzy

Hitchcock rebounded from the triple disappointment of *The Birds*, *Torn Curtain*, and *Topaz* with the 1972 thriller *Frenzy*, a critical and commercial hit. He filmed it in London—it was his first major working visit home since *Stage Fright* in 1950—and filled it with generous amounts of wit, irony, intrigue, and savagery.

The film begins on a bank of the River Thames, where those enjoying a sunny day are jolted by the sight of a woman's corpse floating downstream, naked except for a strip of fabric wrapped around her neck. No doubt about it, the Necktie Murderer has struck again.

We now meet Richard Blaney (Jon Finch), an ill-tempered chap who earns a meager living as a bartender. Fired for cadging brandy on the job, he approaches his ex-wife Brenda (Barbara Leigh-Hunt) for a loan, but his plea turns into a tirade and an ugly quarrel, some of which is overheard by Monica Barling (Jean Marsh), the secretary of the matrimonial agency Brenda runs.

Another key character is Bob Rusk (Barry Foster), a gregarious extrovert who enjoys mixing with the customers at his Covent Garden produce market. He drops in on Brenda's agency the day after her squabble with Richard, demanding that she arrange some sexual companionship for him. She refuses, knowing that his amiable manner hides noxious tastes and foul proclivities. Proving her correct, Bob furiously rapes her on the spot. Then, far worse, he strangles her to death with his tie. We now know the secret all London is desperate to learn—Bob is the Necktie Murderer—but suspicion immediately falls on Richard, who fought with Brenda the previous day.

Enter the story's third key figure, Chief Inspector Oxford (Alec McCowen), a cop whose conscientious work makes him a shining exception to Hitchcock's usual portrayal of the police as irrelevant or obtuse. Oxford too suspects Richard, who's surly and irresponsible, rather than Bob, who's cheery and outgoing. But he's clever enough to look beyond the obvious, and his reasoning ultimately prevails over appearances.

Also in the picture are Richard's loyal girlfriend, Babs Milligan (Anna Massey), and the chief inspector's wife, Mrs. Oxford (Vivien Merchant), an unforgettable spouse who spreads the dinner table with laboriously cooked French dishes that her down-to-earth British husband finds hard to look at, much less eat. Undeterred by blind alleys and red herrings, he finally cracks the Necktie Murderer case, but what seems to please him most is the old-fashioned English breakfast he manages to wolf down at the office.

Frenzy is full of food—not just Inspector Oxford's breakfast and Mrs. Oxford's cordon bleu, but also the fruits and vegetables in Bob's market, the potato-laden truck where he retrieves an incriminating item by breaking the fingers of a corpse he's dumped there, and the bread sticks that Mrs. Oxford snaps in two, inadvertently echoing the sound of the fingers Bob broke in the potato truck. Hitchcock's relationship with eating was both ardent and conflicted, and nowhere did he play out his feelings for foodstuffs with a more intricate blend of hilarity and horror.

My relationship with *Frenzy* has evolved over the years. When it premiered, I had reservations about the obvious red herrings, the broad-brush contrasts between testy Richard and avuncular Bob, and the unsubtle close-ups of Mrs. Oxford's breaking bread sticks. Additional viewings made me more appreciative of the film's deeply embedded Hitchcock themes, including the deceptiveness of appearances, the transfer of guilt from Bob to Richard, and the presence of evil in seemingly sunny surroundings.

I've also come to admire the way Hitchcock didn't try to top the ghastliness of Brenda's murder with an even more appalling scene later in the story, the way most directors would. Instead, he went the other way, confident that after *showing* us Brenda's gruesome death he could make us shudder just as much by simply *indicating* the killer's next crime, which happens behind a closed door while the camera discreetly pulls away. This worked in *Psycho*, where the first murder is crushingly brutal and the second is briefly sketched, and it works again here.

Still and all, I've grown increasingly uncomfortable with the savagery of Brenda's rape and murder. The collapse of Hollywood censorship in the 1960s was clearly liberating for a filmmaker who trafficked in the macabre, and Hitchcock took advantage of it by amping up the violence in *Frenzy* to a degree unrivaled even by Marion's death in *Psycho*, which had seemed almost beyond the pale just a dozen years earlier. The problem isn't that Bob murders Brenda, or that he rapes *and* murders her. What rankles is the visible ferocity of the crime—all the more disturbing in comparison with *Psycho*, which *displays* very little of what Norman's knife is doing in the shower, presenting so many shots at such a slashing speed that the impression of explicit mayhem far outstrips what the spectator actually sees.

Frenzy is vastly different, and the difference is underscored by the last shot of Brenda after her violation and killing are complete: vanquished in body and obliterated in spirit, she gazes at the camera with lifeless eyes, her twisted tongue protruding from her mouth in a last grimace at an uncomprehending and incomprehensible world. In terms of humanist morality, gender politics, aesthetic judgment, and simple taste, all this is hard to watch and difficult to defend. Hitchcock's films are a far, far cry from the feminist nightmares simplistically decried by some commentators, but in this part of *Frenzy*, those commentators have a point.

Such things didn't keep moviegoers away from *Frenzy*, which renewed Hitchcock's popularity and revitalized his reputation. And whatever you think of the picture, you have to admit it has a catchier title than the 1966 novel by Arthur La Bern that inspired it, *Goodbye Piccadilly, Farewell Leicester Square*. Hitch's promotional genius strikes again!

Family Plot

After the grim humor, grim irony, and grim *grimness* of *Frenzy*, it was refreshing to discover that Hitchcock's 53rd and final film, *Family Plot*, had a mellow tone signaled at the start by its Hitchcockian title—two everyday words forming a folksy pun with a sly hint of the macabre. The picture's ingredients are sinister, but after simmering in Hitch's cauldron, they come out as a tasty confection, if not a particularly memorable one.

For a plot synopsis, here's a slightly modified excerpt from my review for *The Christian Science Monitor* in April 1976:

> It all begins with a pretty clairvoyant who isn't really clairvoyant, though she puts on a good show for her credulous clients. Her boyfriend is a taxi driver who wants to be an actor but ends up impersonating a lawyer so he can find the whereabouts of a missing man so the phony clairvoyant can collect a commission from the batty aunt who wants to bequeath her fortune to a nephew she hasn't seen since the family chauffeur smuggled him into … et cetera.
>
> And that's only the beginning. There's another whole plot about a wealthy kidnaper who snatches, among others, a bishop right in the middle of a well-attended church service…. *Family Plot* doesn't make you think very hard

[and doesn't] generate hard-core suspense, but it certainly keeps you on your toes as one episode dovetails neatly with another for nearly two jigsaw-puzzling hours.[26]

The cast includes Barbara Harris as Blanche Tyler, the bogus psychic; Bruce Dern as George Lumley, the cab driver; William Devane as Arthur Adamson, a jeweler turned kidnapper; Karen Black as Frances, his girlfriend and accomplice; Ed Lauter as Joseph Maloney, a small-timer who once helped George with a major scam; Katherine Helmond as Mrs. Maloney, his wife; and Cathleen Nesbitt as Julia Rainbird, a rich old lady who seeks out Blanche's services.

Hitchcock was heading into his late 70s when *Family Plot* premiered. Still an active force in the movie world, he didn't think of this as the last picture he'd be able to complete, but he obviously knew he was getting old, and his physical and emotional health underwent drastic swings while *Family Plot* was in the works; biographer Donald Spoto reports that he was edgy, irascible, and "more ambivalent about making this … than about any picture in years."[27]

Yet he was still highly engaged. He gave detailed instructions on dialogue, camera angles, and everything else, and I think he regarded *Family Plot* as a sort of last stand against frailty, finality, and mortality. It was a quixotic last stand, to be sure, but looking for loopholes in the human condition was nothing new for Hitchcock, who disliked definitive conclusions and always reveled in ambiguities, uncertainties, and shadows of philosophical doubt.

Ambiguity and uncertainty are the qualities that make Hitch's films so open to multiple interpretations, and existential playfulness runs especially strong in *Family Plot*. As the title indicates, the picture has a cemetery at its center, and at one point Mrs. Maloney barges into it, approaches a counterfeit gravestone—Blanche's second sight isn't the only bogus thing in the story—and cries *"Fake! Fake!"* while lustily kicking it. This is surely a character close to Hitchcock's aging heart.

And so is Blanche, who closes the picture with a quintessentially Hitchcockian gesture. Turning directly to the camera, to the director behind it, and to the audience looking on, she gives a deliciously mischievous wink. The final moment of his final film is an apt capstone for Hitchcock's unparalleled career.

8

Epilogue

Hitchcock was planning what would have been his 54th feature, a long-contemplated thriller called *The Short Night*, when he died at 80 of renal failure on April 19, 1980, in Los Angeles. Earlier in the year, Queen Elizabeth had knighted him, an honor he cherished. Among the long list of other honors, prizes, and awards he'd received, the most glaring absence was an Academy Award for best director. But his brilliance as an artist, entertainer, performer, and icon were well known to moviegoers all over the world.

Although the lightly macabre *Family Plot* is not one of the greatest Hitchcock films, its value as a sort of valedictory address to his countless admirers is confirmed by the remarkable number of references it contains to a wide range of pictures spanning much of his career. Some are obvious: when Blanche and George have a wild automobile ride, for instance, it's as darkly comical as Roger Thornhill's perilous drive in *North by Northwest*; and when George pursues an investigation that somewhat recalls the hero's quest in *Vertigo*, the name he invents for a nonexistent law firm is Ferguson, Ferguson and McBride, clearly tipping a hat to Scottie Ferguson in the earlier film.

Other allusions are subtler. Maloney says he's not a "sponger," using a significant word from *Blackmail*. A burning match near a gasoline pump brings *The Birds* to mind. A villain is honored by a misguided funeral speech, as Uncle Charlie is in *Shadow of a Doubt*. And references to *Psycho* abound: Arthur waits for Frances near Bates Avenue; we see a gravestone reading "Mother" when the cemetery scene begins; the whole story is set in motion by a woman—a Rainbird ancestor whose spirit Blanche claims to communicate with—exerting influence from beyond the grave; and George's search for Blanche recalls Lila's search for Marion in the Bates residence, which also culminates in a small chamber in the nether parts of the house.

It's fitting that Hitchcock's last picture takes pleasure in remembering earlier works. Many of his films, from *The 39 Steps* and *The Lady Vanishes* to *Spellbound* and *Marnie*, reflect his belief that memory can defend against the future by reconjuring the past, and his memory circuits were evidently in overdrive when he made *Family Plot*, realizing that his powers were weakening in ways not likely to be reversed. Ernest Lehman, who wrote *North by Northwest* and *Family Plot,* as well as a draft of *The Short Night*, told me in the late 1970s that his working sessions on *Family Plot* were so full of Hitchcock's good-old-days storytelling that getting down to business was often difficult to do.

Movies are excellent memory machines, capturing moments on the fly and preserving them in forms that will be accessible and retrievable as long as moving-image technologies endure. Hitchcock participated in one of history's most important memory exercises immediately after World War II, when he and his partner Sidney Bernstein supervised the editing of footage shot by camera crews accompanying Allied troops who liberated Nazi extermination camps in 1945. The compilation was not publicly shown, but the footage has since been incorporated in the *Frontline* television episode *Memory of the Camps* (PBS, 1985) and a somewhat longer 2014 documentary of the same title. Memory was sometimes a laughing matter for Hitchcock—think of the audience amused by Mr. Memory's mnemonic feats in *The 39 Steps*—but it could be deadly serious as well. The first words we hear from Blanche's familiar spirit in *Family Plot* bear this out: "Too many memories, too much pain, too much sorrow."

Alfred Hitchcock's career traveled to rough, rocky valleys as well as splendid, shining peaks, but ultimately his body of work stands with the most intelligent, sophisticated, and entertaining accomplishments in the history of film. Looking at the blue and scarlet threads of innocence and guilt, morality and crime, good and evil that weave such intricate webs through his 53 completed features, you can easily repeat his own comment about *Strangers on a Train*: "Isn't it a fascinating design? One could study it forever."

Notes

Preface

[1] With a total running time of 198 minutes, *Lost and Found: American Treasures from the New Zealand Film Archive* also includes John Ford's dramatic comedy *Upstream* (1927), about residents of a theatrical boarding house; the short comedy *Won in a Cupboard* (1914), directed by Mabel Normand, who also stars; Howard M. Mitchell's *The Love Charm* (1928), a dramatic short showing sea and sand in the two-color Technicolor process; plus newsreels, a 1920 documentary explaining how Stetson hats are made, an episode from Walter Edwin's serial *Dolly of the Dailies* (1914), a 1923 cartoon, and other vintage entertainments.

[2] Alfred Hitchcock, "*Rear Window*." *Take One* 2, no. 2 (November-December 1968), pp. 18-20. Reprinted in Sidney Gottlieb, ed., *Hitchcock on Hitchcock: Selected Writings and Interviews, Volume 2* (Oakland: University of California Press, 2015), pp. 95-101, cited at p. 99.

[3] Ken Mogg, *The Alfred Hitchcock Story* (London: Titan Books, 1999), p. 101.

[4] François Truffaut with the Collaboration of Helen G. Scott, *Hitchcock*, revised edition. (New York: Simon & Schuster, 1984), pp. 99, 102.

[5] Quoted by British Film Institute (13 August 2013) http://britishfilminstitute.tumblr.com/post/58163387252/for-me-the-cinema-is-not-a-slice-of-life-but-a.

Chapter 1 – Hitch

[1] See for example *The Men Who Made the Movies: Alfred Hitchcock*, an episode of a seven-part television series directed by Richard Schickel and broadcast on PBS in 1973.

[2] See for instance Robin Wood, *Hitchcock's Films Revisited* (New York: Columbia University Press, 1989), pp. 84, 145, 199.

[3] Anne Martinetti & François Riveière, *La Sauce était presque parfaite. 80 recettes d'après Alfred Hitchcock* [*The Sauce Was Almost Perfect: 80 Recipes based on Alfred Hitchcock*] (Paris: Cahiers de Cinéma, 2008). The punning title refers to *Le Crime était presque parfait* [*The Crime Was Almost Perfect*], the French title of *Dial M for Murder*. Martinetti and Riveière also wrote *Crèmes & châtiments: Recettes délicieuses et criminelles* [*Creams and Misdemeanors: The Delicious and Sinful Recipes of Agatha Christie*] (Paris: Le Masque, 2010) and Martinette wrote *Alimentaire mon cher Watson* [*Elementary My Dear Watson*] (Paris: Chne, 2010). Each of these books has photographs by Philippe Asset, self-described "culinary photographer."

[4] Truffaut, *Hitchcock*, p. 47.

[5] Maurice Yacowar, *Hitchcock's British Films* (Detroit: Wayne State University Press, 2010), pp. 33-34.

[6] "A Talk with Hitchcock" (1964), episode directed by Fletcher Markle for the Canadian documentary series *Telescope* (CBC Television, 1963-73).

[7] *Under Capricorn* started as a similar experiment but turned into a somewhat more conventional film when Hitchcock's high hopes for the innovative method failed to materialize. Even these films embody the essence of Kuleshov's theory, thanks to Hitchcock's ability to place contrasting or conflicting elements *within* a single frame.

[8] Tom Ryall, *Alfred Hitchcock & the British Cinema* (Urbana: University of Illinois Press, 1986), p. 177.

[9] Donald Spoto, *The Dark Side of Genius: The Life of Alfred Hitchcock* (Boston: Little, Brown and Company, 1983), pp. 68-69.

[10] "John Player Lecture," in Gottlieb, *Hitchcock on Hitchcock, Volume 2*, pp. 236-257, cited at p. 249.

[11] Spoto, *Dark Side of Genius*, p. 68

[12] Patrick McGilligan, *Alfred Hitchcock: A Life in Darkness and Light* (New York ReganBooks, 2003), p. 50.

[13] Josephine Botting, "Will the real Mrs Hitchcock please stand up?" *BFI* (11 February 2014) http://www.bfi.org.uk/news-opinion/bfi-news/features/will-real-mrs-hitchcock-please-stand-up (retrieved. 22 March 2014).

[14] Charles Champlin, "Alma Reville Hitchcock – The Unsung Partner." *Los Angeles Times* (July 29, 1982), pt. VI, p. 7.

[15] Charlotte Chandler, *It's Only a Movie: Alfred Hitchcock, a Personal Biography* (New York: Applause, 2006), pp. 43-44.

Chapter 2 – Silents Are Golden

[1] Christine Gledhill, "Cutts, Graham (1885-1958)." *BFI ScreenOnline* http://www.screenonline.org.uk/people/id/457310/ (retrieved 16 May 2015).

[2] Alfred Hitchcock, *Stage* (July 1936). Quoted in McGilligan, *Alfred Hitchcock*, p. 754.

[3] Michael Balcon, *Michael Balcon Presents...A Lifetime of Films* (London: Hutchinson, 1969). Quoted in McGilligan, *Alfred Hitchcock*, p. 754.

[4] *Variety* (November 3, 1926). Quoted in McGilligan, *Alfred Hitchcock*, p. 756.

[5] *Pictures and Picturegoer* (October 1924) and *Variety* (May 27, 1925). Quoted in McGilligan, *Alfred Hitchcock*, p. 755.

[6] Mark Duguid, "*The Mountain Eagle*." *BFI* http://old.bfi.org.uk/

nationalarchive/news/mostwanted/mountain-eagle.html (retrieved 16 May 2015).

[7] Marie Belloc Lowndes, *The Lodger*, ed. Elyssa Warkentin (Newcastle upon Tyne: Cambridge Scholars Publishing, 2015). Belloc Lowndes first wrote "The Lodger" as a short story for *McClure's Magazine* (vol. 36, January 1911, pp. 266-77), and the novel followed two years later (London: Methuen, 1913). She also collaborated with the writer Horace Annesley Vachell on a light-comedy stage adaptation of *The Lodger* titled *Who Is He?* It opened in 1916 in London, where Hitchcock saw it, and the following year in New York, where it starred Lionel Atwill and garnered mixed reviews.

[8] Spoto, *Dark Side of Genius*, p. 84.

[9] Spoto, *Dark Side of Genius*, 85.

[10] Review, "The Lodger." *Bioscope* (16 September 1926), p. 39.

[11] Spoto, *Dark Side of Genius*, 95.

[12] Ryall, *Alfred Hitchcock & the British Cinema*, pp. 92-93.

[13] Charles Morgan, "*The Ring*," *The New York Times* (25 December 1927) http://nyti.ms/2v8TomM. Review, "*The Ring*." *Variety* (31 December 1926) http://variety.com/1926/film/reviews/the-ring-1200409812/

[14] Jonathan Rosenbaum, "*The Ring*." *Monthly Film Bulletin* vol. 43 no. 510 (July 1976) http://www.jonathanrosenbaum.net/1976/07/the-ring-1976-review/. GA, "*The Ring*." *Time Out* (20 March 2012) http://www.timeout.com/london/film/the-ring-1.

[15] Noel Coward, *Easy Virtue: A Play in Three Acts* (New York: Harper & Brothers, 1926).

Chapter 3 – Talkies, Theatricality, and the Low Ebb
[1] Truffaut, *Hitchcock*, p. 61.

[2] Leonard J. Leff, *Hitchcock and Selznick: The Rich and Strange Collaboration of Alfred Hitchcock and David O. Selznick in Hollywood.* (New York: Weidenfeld & Nicolson, 1987), p. 11.

[3] Tania Modleski, "Rape vs Mans/laughter: Hitchcock's *Blackmail* and Feminist Interpretation." *PMLA* vol. 102 no. 3 (May 1987), pp. 304-15. Reprinted in slightly different form as the first chapter in Tania Modleski, *The Women Who Knew Too Much: Hitchcock and Feminist Theory*, second ed. (New York: Routledge, 2005).

[4] Truffaut, *Hitchcock*, p. 69.

[5] Clemence Dane and Helen Simpson, *Enter Sir John*, illustrated by Sydney Seymour Lucas (New York: Grosset & Dunlap, 1928).

[6] John Galsworthy, *The Skin Game (A Tragicomedy)* (Oxford, MS: Project Gutenberg, 2001) http://manybooks.net/titles/galswortetext01skgam11.html# (retrieved 4 February 2015).

[7] Mordaunt Hall, "A College Romance. A Galsworthy Play. Fashionable Flirtations. A German Musical Film. Teutonic Fun." *The New York Times* (20 June 1931) http://nyti.ms/2uaZ0A0 (retrieved 22 June 2015)

[8] Truffaut, *Hitchcock*, p. 77.

[9] William Shakespeare, *The Tempest*, ed. Barbara A. Mowat and Paul Werstine (New York: Washington Square Press, 1994), p. 41.

[10] Mark Duguid, "*Number Seventeen* (1932)." *BFI ScreenOnline* (n.d.) http://www.screenonline.org.uk/film/id/437945/ (retrieved 10 October 2015).

[11] Michael Brooke, "*Waltzes from Vienna* (1933). *BFI ScreenOnline* (n.d.) http://www.screenonline.org.uk/film/id/442476/ (retrieved 10 October 2015).

[12] Truffaut, *Hitchcock*, p. 87.

Chapter 4 – The Classic Thriller Sextet

[1] The classic thriller sextet was so named by Raymond Durgnat in *The Strange Case of Alfred Hitchcock, or The Plain Man's Hitchcock* (Cambridge, MA: MIT Press, 1974), p. 20.

[2] Ryall, *Alfred Hitchcock & the British Cinema*, p. 118.

[3] *The Man Who Knew Too Much* is so described by Kent Jones in the 2015 film *Hitchcock/Truffaut*, a coproduction of Arte France, Artline Films, and Cohen Media Group, directed by Jones, written by Jones and Serge Toubiana.

[4] Staff, "*The Man Who Knew Too Much*." *Variety* (31 December 1934) http://variety.com/1934/film/reviews/the-man-who-knew-too-much-1200410948/ (retrieved 9 June 2015).

[5] A.S., "*The Man Who Knew Too Much* At the Mayfair (23 March 1935) http://nyti.ms/2u23lp0 (retrieved 9 June 2015).

[6] John Buchan, *The Thirty-Nine Steps* (Mineola, NY: Dover Publications, 1994).

[7] Joseph Conrad, *The Secret Agent: A Simple Tale* (New York: Signet Classics, 1983).

[8] W. Somerset Maughan, *Ashenden or: The British Agent* (New Brunswick, NJ: Transaction Publishers, 2010).

[9] Maugham, *Ashenden*, p. 289.

[10] Their last film as cowriters was Robert Day's *The Green Man* in 1956; their last as codirectors was *The Great St. Trinian's Train Robbery* in 1966. Gilliat retired after writing, directing, and coproducing the Agatha Christie adaptation *Endless Night* in 1972. Launder retired after writing and directing *The Wildcats of St. Trinian's*, the fifth film in the *St. Trinian's* franchise, in 1980.

[11] Exceptions are *The Man Who Knew Too Much*, where the main

characters are married all along, and where the source is not a novel but an original scenario by Edwin Greenwood and A.R. Rawlinson inspired by the then-popular Bulldog Drummond books and movies; *The Lady Vanishes*, which Bennett did not write; *Secret Agent*, which takes place two decades before the film was made; and *Young and Innocent*, which has no detectable political edge. Charles Barr, *English Hitchcock* (Moffat, Scotland: Cameron & Hollis, 1999).

[12] *The 39 Steps* was remade by Ralph Thomas in 1959, with Kenneth More as Hannay, and Patrick Barlow's comic-melodramatic stage adaptation has won applause and awards on Broadway and elsewhere. Other movies of this title, taking their main cues from Buchan's novel rather than Hitchcock's film, have been directed by Don Sharp (1978, with Robert Powell, David Warner, and John Mills) and James Hawes (2008, with Rupert Perry-Jones and Eddie Marsan).

[13] Truffaut, *Hitchcock*, p. 123.

Chapter 5 – Hollywood
[1] I borrow the phrase "total filmmaker" from the title of Jerry Lewis's book about his craft, comprising edited versions of lectures he gave at the University of Southern California starting in 1967. The term suits Hitchcock far better than it suits Lewis, fascinating though the latter is in his way. Jerry Lewis, *The Total Film-Maker* (New York: Random House, 1971).

[2] D.W. Griffith, Charles Chaplin, Cecil B. DeMille, King Vidor, John Ford, Frank Capra, Ernst Lubitsch, and Howard Hawks were among their number.

[3] "Code of Credits – Theatrical Motion Pictures." *Producers Guild of America* (n.d.) http://www.producersguild.org/?page=coc_tmp (retrieved 12 May 2015).

[4] McGilligan, *Alfred Hitchcock*, p. 160.

[5] Jan Olsson, *Hitchcock à la Carte* (Durham, NC: Duke University Press, 2015), p. 13.

[6] Alfred Hitchcock, "Directors Are Dead." *Film Weekly* (20 November 1937), p. 14. Reprinted in Sidney Gottlieb, ed., *Hitchcock on Hitchcock: Selected Writings and Interviews* (Berkeley: University of California Press, 1995), 183–85, cited at 184–85. See also Olsson, *Hitchcock à la Carte*, pp. 118–19.

[7] Hitchcock, "Directors Are Dead,"pp. 185, 184.

[8] McGilligan, *Alfred Hitchcock*, p. 379. Leff, *Hitchcock and Selznick*, p. 218.

[9] Daphne du Maurier, *Rebecca* (New York: Harper, 2006), p. 1.

[10] Matthew Dennison, "How Daphne du Maurier wrote *Rebecca*." *The Telegraph* (19 April 2008) http://www.telegraph.co.uk/culture/books/3672739/How-Daphne-du-Maurier-wrote-Rebecca.html (retrieved 4 May 2015).

[11] V.S. Pritchett, "Daphne du Maurier Writes a Victorian Thriller – A London Letter." *The Christian Science Monitor* (9 September 1938), p. WM12.

[12] Ronald Haver, *David O. Selznick's Hollywood* (Los Angeles: Bonanza Books, 1980), p. 324.

[13] Thomas Schatz, *The Genius of the System: Hollywood Filmmaking in the Studio Era* (New York: Henry Holt and Company, 1996), p. 284.

[14] Vincent Sheean, *Personal History* (New York: Doubleday, 1935).

[15] James Naremore, "*Foreign Correspondent:* The Windmills of War." *Current* (18 February 2014) https://www.criterion.com/current/posts/3063-foreign-correspondent-the-windmills-of-war. My discussion draws in part on Naremore's essay, which accompanies The Criterion Collection edition of the film released on DVD and Blu-ray in 2014.

[16] Naremore, "*Foreign Correspondent.*"

[17] Allardyce Nicoll, *A History of Restoration Drama* (New York: Cambridge University Press, 1923), p. 185. Cited in Joy Gould

Boyum, "Columbia's Screwball Comedies: Wine, Women, and Wisecracks," in Bernard F. Dick, ed., *Columbia Pictures: Portrait of a Studio* (Lexington: The University Press of Kentucky, 2010), pp. 89–105, cited at p. 91.

[18] Cavell's examples include Frank Capra's *It Happened One Night* (1934), Howard Hawks's *Bringing Up Baby* (1938) and *His Girl Friday* (1940), Preston Sturges's *The Lady Eve* (1941), and George Cukor's *The Philadelphia Story* (1940) and *Adam's Rib* (1949). See Stanley Cavell, *Pursuits of Happiness: The Hollywood Comedy of Remarriage* (Cambridge, MA: Harvard University Press, 1981).

[19] Truffaut, *Hitchcock*, p. 139.

[20] Spoto, *Dark Side of Genius*, pp. 237–239.

[21] Truffaut, *Hitchcock*, p. 142.

[22] Bill Krohn, Revisions to "Bill Krohn on *Suspicion*." *Alfred Hitchcock Scholars/"MacGuffin"* (17 October 2003) http://www.labyrinth.net.au/~muffin/suspicion_c..html#Middle (retrieved 9 February 2016).

[23] "*Saboteur*: Notes." *TCM* (n.d.) http://www.tcm.com/tcmdb/title/ 88836/Saboteur/notes.html (retrieved 2 February 2016).

[24] Bosley Crowther, "*Saboteur*, Alfred Hitchcock Melodrama, Starring Priscilla Lane, Robert Cummings and Otto Kruger, at Music Hall." *The New York Times* (8 May 1942) http://nyti.ms/2ub0Pg3; "The New Pictures." *Time* (11 May 1942), quoted in "*Saboteur*," *TCM* (n.d.) http://www.tcm.com/tcmdb/title/88836/Saboteur/articles.html; "Review: *Saboteur*." *Variety* (31 December 1941) http://variety.com/ 1941/film/reviews/saboteur-1200413820/; Powell quoted in Leff, *Hitchcock and Selznick*, p. 102; Pauline Kael, "*Saboteur*," in *5001 Nights at the Movies: A guide from A to Z* (New York: Holt, Rinehart and Winston, 1982), p. 508. (Web materials retrieved 9 February 2016).

[25] Jack Sullivan, *Hitchcock's Music* (New Haven: Yale University Press, 2006), p. 104.

[26] "Review: *Lifeboat.*" *Variety* (31 December 1943) http://variety.com/1943/film/reviews/lifeboat-1200414278/; Thompson quoted in Spoto, *Dark Side of Genius*, p. 269; Bosley Crowther, "*Lifeboat*, a Film Picturization of Shipwrecked Survivors, With Tallulah Bankhead, Opens at the Astor Theatre." *The New York Times* (13 January 1944) http://nyti.ms/2uaXsG0. (Website materials retrieved 9 February 2016).

[27] Hitchcock also did uncredited work on two other public-affairs shorts around this time: *The Fighting Generation* (1944, USA, with Jennifer Jones and Rhonda Fleming, 2 minutes) and *Watchtower Over Tomorrow* (1945, USA, with Lionel Stander, George Zucco, and John Nesbitt, 15 minutes).

[28] David Sterritt, "Hitchcock Work Resurfaces." *The Christian Science Monitor* (14 July 1993) http://www.csmonitor.com/1993/0714/14131.html (retrieved 9 February 2016).

[29] Leonard Leff, "Selznick International's *Spellbound.*" *Current* (23 September 2002) https://www.criterion.com/current/posts/223-selznick-international-s-spellbound (Retrieved 14 November 2015).

[30] Truffaut, *Hitchcock*, p. 165.

[31] Matthew H. Bernstein, "Unrecognizable Origins: 'The Song of the Dragon' and *Notorious*, in R. Barton Palmer and David Boyd, eds., *Hitchcock at the Source: The Auteur as Adaptor* (Albany: SUNY Press, 2011), pp. 139-158, cited at p. 152.

[32] "*Notorious*," in Alan Gevinson, ed., *American Film Institute Catalog – Within Our Gates: Ethnicity in American Feature Films, 1911-1960* (Berkeley: University of California Press, 1997), pp. 728-29, cited at p. 729.

[33] Truffaut, *Hitchcock*, p. 174.

[34] Spoto, *Dark Side of Genius*, p. 294.

[35] Truffaut, *Hitchcock*, pp. 173, 177.

[36] Leff, *Hitchcock and Selznick*, pp. 261-262.

[37] Bill Krohn, *Hitchcock at Work* (London: Phaidon Press, 2003), p. 114.

[38] Patrick Hamilton, *Rope: A Play*. London: French, 2003.

[39] Michael Shermer, "Creationism," in Michael Shermer, ed., *The Skeptic Encyclopedia of Pseudoscience*, vol. 2 (Santa Barbara: ABC-CLIO, 2002), p. 776.

[40] Truffaut, *Hitchcock*, p. 182.

[41] Lindsay Anderson, "Alfred Hitchcock." *Sequence* 9 (Autumn 1949). Reprinted in Albert J. LaValley, ed., *Focus on Hitchcock* (Englewood Cliffs, NJ: Prentice-Hall, 1972), 48–59, cited at 57.

[42] Truffaut, *Hitchcock*, pp. 180, 184.

[43] Spoto, *Dark Side of Genius*, p. 310.

Chapter 6 – The Fabulous 1950s

[1] Doubleday published Jepson's novel, *Outrun the Constable*, in 1947, after it had been serialized in *Collier's* under the title *Man Running*. Bantam reprinted it under a third title, *Killer by Proxy*, in 1950.

[2] Krohn, *Hitchcock at Work*, p. 111.

[3] Truffaut, *Hitchcock*, p. 189.

[4] Rudyard Kipling, "If –," in Rudyard Kipling, *Rewards and Fairies* (Garden City, NY: Doubleday, 1910), pp. 181-182, cited at p. 181.

[5] Staff writer, "Review: *Strangers on a Train.*" *Variety* (31 December 1950) http://variety.com/1950/film/reviews/strangers-on-a-train-1200416895/.

[6] Krohn, *Hitchcock at Work*, p. 114.

[7] Truffaut, *Hitchcock*, p. 195.

[8] For convenience, I refer to them as Bruno and Guy, the first names used in the film.

[9] Charles Thomas Samuels, "Alfred Hitchcock," in Charles Thomas Samuels, *Encountering Directors* (New York: G.P. Putnam's Sons, 1972, pp. 231-250, cited at p. 244. Also cited in Sidney Gottlieb, ed., *Alfred Hitchcock: Interviews* (Jackson: University Press of Mississippi, 2003), pp. 119-155, cited at p. 149.

[10] Colin Marshall, "Raymond Chandler Denounces *Strangers on a Train* in Sharply-Worded Letter to Alfred Hitchcock." *Open Culture* (29 August 2013) http://www.openculture.com/2013/08/raymond-chandler-denounces-hitchcocks-strangers-on-a-train.html (retrieved 7 March 2015).

[11] Chandler nevertheless has screen credit with Ormonde as coauthor of the screenplay, thanks to Warner's high regard for famous names that might bring fans to the ticket window.

[12] Krohn, *Hitchcock at Work*, p. 118.

[13] Paul Anthelme, *Nos deux consciences: Pièce en cinq actes, en prose* (Paris: L'Illustration, 1902). Paul Anthelme was the *nom de plume* of Paul Bourde, a French dramatist, journalist, and colonialist. The play was published as a supplement to *L'Illustration* a week after its Paris premiere. See also Paul Bourde, *Our Two Consciences: Drama in Five Acts*, trans. Morry C. Matson (CreateSpace Independent Publishing Platform, 2013).

[14] Caroline Moorehead, *Sidney Bernstein: A Biography* (London: Jonathan Cape, 1984), p. 194.

[15] Knott, Frederick. *Dial "M" for Murder: A Collage for Voices*. New York: Dramatists Play Service, 1953.

[16] Chandler, *It's Only a Movie*, p. 207.

[17] Truffaut, *Hitchcock*, p. 213.

[18] Chandler, *It's Only a Movie*, p. 207.

[19] Krohn, *Hitchcock at Work*, p. 130.

[20] *The Creature from the Black Lagoon* was another last-ditch 3D attraction, preceding Hitchcock's film by about three months. J. Hoberman, "The Stunt Men." *The Village Voice* (6 April 1999) http://www.villagevoice.com/film/the-stunt-men-6422095 (retrieved 9 May 2015).

[21] McGilligan, *Alfred Hitchcock*, pp. 479, 483-4.

[22] Walter Raubicheck and Walter Srebnick, eds., *Hitchcock's Rereleased Films: From* Rope *to* Vertigo (Detroit: Wayne State University Press, 1991), pp. 19-20.

[23] I've corrected Canby's misspelling (Jeffries) of Jefferies's name. Vincent Canby, "*Rear Window* – Still a Joy." *The New York Times* (9 October 1983) http://nyti.ms/2v9khai (retrieved 9 May 2015).

[24] Woolrich published "It Had to Be Murder" in the February 1942 issue of *Dime Detective Magazine* under his pseudonym William Irish.

[25] David Sterritt, "Hitchcock's genius on view in *Window*." *The Christian Science Monitor* (21 January 2000) http://www.csmonitor.com/2000/0121/p15s1.html (retrieved 9 May 2015).

[26] Bosley Crowther, Cat Man Out *To Catch a Thief*; Grant Is Ex-

Burglar in Hitchcock Thriller." *The New York Times* (5 August 1955) http://nyti.ms/2u2gVsr (retrieved 9 May 2015).

[27] This was Burks's only Oscar; two of his three additional nominations were for the Hitchcock films *Strangers on a Train* and *Rear Window*.

[28] Pauline Kael, "*To Catch a Thief*," in Kael, *5001 Nights at the Movies*, p. 604.

[29] David Sterritt, *The Films of Alfred Hitchcock* (New York: Cambridge University Press, 1993), pp. 25-6.

[30] "I am but mad north-north-west. When the wind is southerly I know a hawk from a handsaw." William Shakespeare, *The Tragical History of Hamlet, Prince of Denmark* (London: Arden Shakespeare, 2006), p. 261.

Chapter 7 – From *Psycho* to *Family Plot*
[1] Robert Bloch, *Psycho* (New York: Tor, 1959), p. 51.

[2] Stephen Rebello, *Alfred Hitchcock and the Making of Psycho* (New York: Dembner Books, 1990), p. 13.

[3] Rebello, *Alfred Hitchcock and the Making of Psycho*, p. 26.

[4] Rebello, *Alfred Hitchcock and the Making of Psycho*, p. 165.

[5] Bosley Crowther, "*Psycho*." *The New York Times* (17 June 1960) http://nyti.ms/2uaZCFP (retrieved 3 February 2016).

[6] Robert E. Kapsis, *Hitchcock: The Making of a Reputation* (Chicago: The University of Chicago Press, 1992), p. 63.

[7] Rebello, *Alfred Hitchcock and the Making of Psycho*, p. 164.

[8] Daphne du Maurier, "The Birds." *Good Housekeeping* (October 1952), pp. 54-55, 110-32. The story then appeared in Daphne du Maurier, *The Apple Tree: A Short Novel and Several Long Stories*

(London: Victor Gollancz, 1952). *The Apple Tree* was published in the US as *Kiss Me Again, Stranger; A Collection of Eight Stories Long and Short* (New York: Doubleday, 1953) with two stories not in the British edition. Republished as *The Birds and Other Stories* (London: Penguin, 1963).

[9] Patrick McGrath, "Mistress of Menace." *The Guardian* (4 May 2007) https://www.theguardian.com/books/2007/may/05/ fiction.daphnedumaurier (retrieved 3 February 2016).

[10] Evan Hunter, *Me and Hitch* (London: Faber and Faber, 1997).

[11] Charles L.P. Silet, "Writing for Hitchcock: An Interview with Ed McBain." *MysteryNet* (n.d.) http://www.mysterynet.com/hitchcock/ mcbain/ (retrieved 9 February 2016). Hunter has written many crime and mystery novels under the pseudonym, Ed McBain.

[12] *Variety*, "*The Birds*." (31 December 1962) http://variety.com/1962/ film/reviews/the-birds-1200420325/ (retrieved 9 February 2016).

[13] Kapsis, *Hitchcock*, p. 93.

[14] Steve Lensman, "*The Birds* (1963)." *Hub Pages* (11 November 2015) (retrieved 9 February 2016). http://hubpages.com/entertainment/The-Birds-1963-Illustrated-Reference.

[15] Bosley Crowther, "*The Birds*: Hitchcock's Feathered Fiends are Chilling." *The New York Times* (1 April 1963) http://www.nytimes.com/library/film/040163hitch-birds-review.html (retrieved 9 February 2016).

[16] Andrew Sarris, "Films." *The Village Voice* (4 April 1963) http://www.villagevoice.com/news/the-birth-of-the-voice-19551965-6401805 (retrieved 9 February 2016).

[17] Tony Lee Moral, *Hitchcock and the Making of "Marnie,"* (Lanham, MA: The Scarecrow Press, p. 30.

[18] Evan Hunter, *Me and Hitch*, pp. 75-6. Emphasis in original.

[19] Murray Pomerance, *An Eye for Hitchcock* (New Brunswick: Rutgers University Press, 2004), p. 284.

[20] Eugene Archer, "Hitchcock's *Marnie*, With Tippi Hedren and Sean Connery." *New York Times* (23 July 1964) http://nyti.ms/ 2v8UqiD (retrieved 26 February 2016).

[21] Andrew Sarris, *Confessions of a Cultist: On the Cinema, 1955-1969* (New York: Simon and Schuster, 1970), pp. 141-44, cited at 141, 144. Originally in *The Village Voice* (9 July 1964).

[22] Jeff Stafford, "*Marnie* (1964)." *TCM* (n.d.) http://www.tcm.com/ tcmdb/title/19882/Marnie/articles.html (retrieved 26 February 2016).

[23] Tim Hunter, "*Torn Curtain*." *The Harvard Crimson* (19 July 1966) http://www.thecrimson.com/article/1966/7/19/torn-curtain-palfred-hitchcock-describes-most/ (retrieved 26 February 2016).

[24] Vincent Canby, "*Topaz*." *The New York Times* (20 December 1969) http://nyti.ms/2u2J8zr (retrieved 26 February 2016).

[25] Richard Corliss, "*Topaz*." *Film Quarterly* vol. 23 no. 3 (Spring 1970) pp. 41-44, cited at 43-4. Richard T. Jameson, "Hitchcock's *Topaz* Revisited." *Parallax View* (30 July 2009) http://parallax-view.org/2009/ 07/30/hitchcock%E2%80%99s-topaz-revisited/. Jameson's essay first appeared in *Helix* (16 April 1970) in somewhat different form. (both citations retrieved 26 February 2016).

[26] David Sterritt, "*Family Plot* is mellow, cheerful, delightful." *The Christian Science Monitor* (29 April 1976), p. 26.

[27] Spoto, *The Dark Side of Genius*, p. 531.

Suggested Reading

More volumes have been devoted to Alfred Hitchcock than to any other filmmaker, ranging from monographs for scholars and specialists to books for movie buffs and general readers. This list suggests a few good places to start, bearing in mind that Hitchcock's rich filmography is sure to inspire countless more studies, appreciations, and critiques in time to come.

Richard Allen and Sidney Gottlieb, eds., *Hitchcock Annual*, published yearly. A thoughtfully and punctiliously edited journal presenting essays on all aspects of Hitchcock's life and work.

Dan Auiler, *Hitchcock's Notebooks: An Authorized and Illustrated Look Inside the Creative Mind of Alfred Hitchcock* (New York Avon, 1999) An assiduous researcher delves into the archives and files for a superbly documented journey through Hitchcock's filmography.

Charles Barr, *English Hitchcock* (Moffat, UK: Cameron & Hollis, 1999) A highly respected scholar focuses on the twenty-three British films made by Hitchcock in the early years of his career.

Lesley Brill, *The Hitchcock Romance: Love and Irony in Hitchcock's Films* (Princeton, NJ: Princeton University Press, 1988). An articulate critic's lucid treatment of Hitchcockian themes related to romance in the broad cultural sense of the term.

Paula Marantz Cohen, *Alfred Hitchcock: The Legacy of Victorianism* (Lexington: University Press of Kentucky, 1995) A versatile scholar traces the influence of Victorian sensibilities in Hitchcock films from multiple stages of his career.

Sidney Gottlieb, ed. *Hitchcock on Hitchcock: Selected Writings and Interviews*, Volumes 1 and 2 (Berkeley: University of California Press, 1995 and 2014). Hitchcock was an able essayist and an eloquent speaker, and these invaluable volumes bring together many of the commentaries he set forth on movies in general and his own movies in particular. Highly recommended.

Alain Kerzoncuf and Charles Barr, *Hitchcock Lost and Found: The Forgotten Films* (Lexington: University Press of Kentucky, 2015) Like many works from cinema's first decades, some of Hitchcock's early films have been partially or entirely lost, and other projects were never completed or even started. This well-written book fills in the picture.

Leonard J. Leff, *Hitchcock and Selznick: The Rich and Strange Collaboration of Alfred Hitchcock and David O. Selznick in Hollywood* (New York: Weidenfeld & Nicolson, 1987). Selznick was a major Hollywood producer when he brought Hitchcock to Hollywood at the end of the 1930s, and the troubles in their relationship didn't diminish the excellence of such joint ventures as *Rebecca* and *Notorious*. This is a gripping account of their brief but fruitful partnership.

Thomas Leitch and Leland Poague, eds., *A Companion to Alfred Hitchcock* (Malden, MA: Wiley-Blackwell, 2011) A wide-ranging collection of essays (including one by this writer) covering all facets of Hitchcock's career.

Patrick McGilligan, *Alfred Hitchcock: A Life in Darkness and Light* (New York: ReganBooks, 2003) A thorough and conscientious biography giving appropriate weight to the good as well as the dubious aspects of Hitchcock's life.

Tania Modleski, *The Women Who Knew Too Much: Hitchcock and Feminist Theory* (New York: Methuen, 1988). A smart, insightful study of women in Hitchcock's films, analyzing the director's sometimes problematic, often surprisingly nuanced treatment of female characters.

Jan Olsson, *Hitchcock à la Carte* (Durham: Duke University Press, 2015) Food, publicity, and television are the main subjects of this very entertaining study by a first-rate critic.

Barton Palmer and David Boyd, eds., *Hitchcock at the Source: The Auteur as Adaptor* (Albany: State University of New York Press, 2011) Twenty essays (including one by this writer) about Hitchcock's use of material borrowed from other sources and transformed to suit his own creative purposes.

Stephen Rebello, *Alfred Hitchcock and the Making of "Psycho"* (New York: Dembner, 1990) *Psycho* is inimitable despite its many imitators, and this is arguably the best of the making-of books inspired by various Hitchcock films.

Donald Spoto, *The Dark Side of Genius: The Life of Alfred Hitchcock* (Boston: Little, Brown, 1983) The first major unauthorized biography of Hitchcock, putting a tad too much emphasis on the unsavory aspects of his personality. Fascinating nonetheless.

François Truffaut with Helen G. Scott, *Hitchcock* (New York: Simon & Schuster, 1984) Hitchcock discusses his movies with another brilliant filmmaker who was one of his most intelligent and scrupulous admirers. This legendary volume, originally published in 1967, is the one truly indispensable "Hitchbook."

Robin Wood, *Hitchcock's Films Revisited* (New York: Columbia University Press, 1989) In this wide-ranging study, which originated as a briefer monograph published in 1965, a perceptive critic comments on Hitchcock's works in astute, sometimes affectingly personal ways.

About the Author

David Sterritt is a film professor at Columbia University and the Maryland Institute College of Art. The author of *The Films of Alfred Hitchcock* (1993), he also serves as the editor of *The Quarterly Review of Film and Video* and is a contributing writer for *Cineaste*. His writing on Hitchcock has appeared in *Film Quarterly*, *Film-Philosophy*, *The Christian Science Monitor* and other periodicals, and he serves on the editorial advisory board of the *Hitchcock Annual*. He recently completed ten years as chair of the National Society of Film Critics.

Afterword

Thank you for reading *Simply Hitchcock*!

If you enjoyed reading it, we would be grateful if you could help others discover and enjoy it too.

Please review it with your favorite book provider such as Amazon, BN, Kobo, iBooks, and Goodreads, among others.

Again, thank you for your support and we look forward to offering you more great reads in the future.

A Note on the Type

Cardo is an Old Style font specifically designed for the needs of classicists, Biblical scholars, medievalists, and linguists. Created by David J. Perry, it was inspired by a typeface cut for the Renaissance printer Aldus Manutius that he first used to print Pietro Bembo's book *De Aetna*, which has been revived in modern times under several names.

CPSIA information can be obtained
at www.ICGtesting.com
Printed in the USA
LVHW032025220419
615089LV00002B/189